# Norfolk & Western Steam:
# The Last 30 Years
## Thomas W. Dixon, Jr.

Published 2013 by
TLC Publishing Inc.
18292 Forest Rd.
Forest, Virginia 24551
434-385-4076
www.greatrailroadbooks.com

ISBN 9780939487639

Library of Congress Control Number: 2013953385

Edited by Rick Van Horn and Karen Parker
Digital Photo Production, Layout and Design by
Karen Parker

Printed in the U.S.A. by
Walsworth Print Group, Marceline, Mo.

*Cover Photo: Y6 No. 2141 poses with an eastbound coal train, displaying the white flags that show that the train is running as an extra (unscheduled train), as all coal trains did on the N&W. The location is the New River Palisades, whose dolomite spires are located near Pembroke, Va. No. 2141 was built at Roanoke in November, 1939, and retired in September, 1960, but in this photo, probably taken in the early 1950s, it is truly the "King of the Road." (N&W photo, TLC Collection, colorized by Karen Parker)*

*Title Page: N&W class Y-6 No. 2135 with a freight train in the Blue Ridge Mountains in June, 1954. (John Krause photo, TLC Collection)*

*Opposite: N&W class A at Reese Station, 5 miles south of Columbus, Ohio, rushes empty coal cars south, back to the coal fields, circa 1950. (Bernard Kern photo, TLC Collection)*

*Back Cover Upper Left: J Class 4-8-4 No. 606 with a passenger train at Crewe, Va. on August 24, 1958. (TLC Collection)*

*Back Cover Upper Right: Y-6b No 2176 with an eastbound freight moves through the yard at Roanoke, Va. in June 1, 1956. (Bob's Photo Collection)*

*Back Cover Lower Left: A pair of Y6 2-8-8-2s lift a manifest freight train up Blueridge Grade on August 7, 1958. (Bob's Photos Collection)*

*Back Cover Lower Right: Y6 with coal train on Elkhorn grade in June, 1959. New diesel helpers are visible in the background. (Gene Huddleston photo, TLC Collection).*

# Table of Contents

# Foreword

This book is intended to present an album of good photos showing steam locomotives operating on the Norfolk & Western Railway in the era 1930-1960. It gives special emphasis to the post-World War II period when N&W was the last hold-out against the inroads of diesel motive power on American railways.

The book is not intended to be a detailed study of the operational or mechanical histories of the various locomotive classes, nor of a history of motive power on the N&W. Enough background data is given in each chapter to show the historical development of the particular class of locomotive being shown and some general roster data. For detailed operational and mechanical histories of the N&W's motive power fleet in the steam era the following books are recommended:

*Norfolk & Western, Giant of Steam*, by Lewis Ingles Jeffries;

*Norfolk & Western, Pocahontas Coal Carrier*, by Richard Prince;

*Norfolk & Western's Class A, Mercedes of Steam*, by Ed King;

*Norfolk & Western Y-Class Articulated Steam Locomotives* by T. W. Dixon, Karen Parker & Gene Huddleston;

*N&W's Shenandoah Valley Line* by Mason Y. Cooper;

*Norfolk & Western Steam, the Last 25 Years* by Ron Rosenberg and Eric H. Archer; and

*Norfolk & Western Class J*, by Kenneth L. Miller.

These are the main books, which, taken together, give a detailed picture of N&W steam operations. Much has also been written in the Norfolk & Western Railway Historical Society's magazine, *The Arrow*. This remains a good continuing source and anyone interested in N&W and N&W motive power should become a member.

The bulk of this book will be about the three major classes that made up the modern N&W steam fleet: Y-Class 2-8-8-2 compound articulateds, A-Class 2-6-6-4 simple articulateds, and J-class 4-8-4s, because they handled the vast majority of N&W's business in this era. These chapters appear at the front of the book. Material about other types and classes appears in the later chapters.

Thanks is extent ended to N&W Historical Society (Bob Bowers) for encouragement in this work, to Ron Rosenberg for assistance with photos and reading for accuracy, Karen Parker who did the layout and design and whose knowledge of steam locomotives is encyclopedic, and to the many photographers, living and dead, whose work appears in these pages.

Thomas W. Dixon, Jr.
Lynchburg, Virginia, August 2013

*N&W class M No. 457 at Kenova, W.Va. 10-3-49. (Charles Felstead photo, TLC Collection)*

# 1: Introduction

The Norfolk & Western Railway in the era 1930–1960 operated about 2,300 miles of first track in Virginia, West Virginia, Kentucky, and Ohio. Its main lines extended from Norfolk, Virginia, to Cincinnati and Columbus, Ohio, and Bristol, Tennessee, while its many branches covered far western Virginia and southern West Virginia, from whence its main revenue came in the form of bituminous coal. A few mines were served across the Tug Fork of the Big Sandy River in Kentucky.

N&W's earliest lineal predecessor was the Norfolk & Petersburg Railroad, begun in 1850. By 1858 it had reached its terminal cities. Beginning in 1854 the Southside Railroad was built between Petersburg and Lynchburg, Virginia, and in 1856 the Virginia & Tennessee reached from Lynchburg to Bristol, Virginia/Tennessee. These lines were important Confederate supply lines during the War Between the States. In 1867 all three were combined into a new consolidated road called the Atlantic, Mississippi & Ohio. Like many southern railroads in the post-war era, its struggled with little capital and its business, based on the largely agrarian countryside through which it ran, was none too lucrative. Then, in 1881 financiers from Philadelphia, who owned the Shenandoah Valley Railroad, a line extending from Hagerstown, Maryland, down the valley to a connection with the AM&O, took control of the later line and renamed it the Norfolk & Western. Its headquarters was established in the new town or Roanoke, in western Virginia at the point where the old AM&O line met the Shenandoah Valley line.

During the post-war era the vast coal resources of the new state of West Virginia were being exploited. The Baltimore & Ohio, in the northern region of the state had been carrying coal since before the war from the fields in that area. Following the war the Chesapeake & Ohio, a line that ran roughly parallel with the new N&W but from Newport News, on the northern side of the Hampton Roads Harbor (whereas N&W ran from Norfolk, on the southern shore) had built across West Virginia in 1873 and reached Cincinnati in 1889. Numerous coal mines opened along C&O's main line and it began to extend branches and to cultivate the coal business, especially after its eastern extension reached Newport News in 1881.

The new managers of N&W obviously wanted to tap the coal reserves of West Virginia and extended its lines into that state, reaching the Ohio River in 1892, where it connected with the Scioto Valley Railroad of Ohio by a large bridge and thus gained connection to Columbus and the many lines feeding the developing industrial Midwest. This was a perfect western outlet for its coal, while the great ice-free port of Hampton Roads provided an ideal eastern terminal, where coal could be shipped to the Northeastern United States via coastwise navigation. N&W also reached Cincinnati by purchase of the Portsmouth & Virginia Railroad in 1901. The Shenandoah Valley line gave N&W a gateway to the northeast through rail connection with the Pennsylvania Railroad (PRR) at Hagerstown, Md.

In fact the PRR became a principal and controlling owner of N&W. The influence of the PRR was most noticeable in the signals that N&W adopted in the later years, but little else associated the two railroads. PRR was interested in N&W as a good investment and as a possible way to enter the South, much as B&O was seeking to do at the same time (with its own Shenandoah Valley line and dabbling in the Kentucky

*The big three of N&W's modern steam were the Y, A, and J classes. For passenger service the streamlined J-class 4-8-4s were among the best of their type as far as their operational capabilities, availability, power, and ability to make long sustained runs. The first five were delivered in 1941, the second group (six engines) came in 1943 and were called freight engines, with no streamlining, to get around war-time restrictions. After the war they were given their streamlined cowls. The last three came in 1950. Here No. 600, the first of the type, is hurrying the* Powhatan Arrow *along the New River at Dry Branch, Virginia on May 7, 1946. (N&W Ry. Photo, TLC Collection)*

Probably the best known, most often reproduced image of N&W freight service in the steam era is a train with one of the line's great 2-8-8-2 Y-class compound articulated locomotives. At home about anywhere on the system and in any service (except passenger) the Y-class locomotives were truly the workhorses of the road. Y-6 No. 2135, built by Raonoke in 1939 is storming up the Blue Ridge grade in Virginia in June 1954 with fast freight. By then auxiliary water tenders were regularly assigned to these leviathans. (John Krause photo, TLC Collection)

coal fields), and as New York Central did through the Big Four and its control of the C&O after 1889. N&W eventually built a large network of coal braches both in southern West Virginia and southwestern Virginia. It built or acquired lines to Winston-Salem and Durham, North Carolina, and a few other areas. In 1909 the Virginian Railway was completed between Deepwater, West Virginia (on the C&O main line) and Norfolk and became a competitor of both N&W and C&O in the eastbound coal business. Both N&W and C&O saw their coal traffic rise both eastward and westward in the succeeding decades. In World War I, when the federal government seized the railroads under the United States Railroad Administration (USRA), it grouped C&O, Virginian, and N&W under a single management and called it the "Pocahontas Region," named for the famous coal seam along the N&W. From then onward the three lines were known as "the Pocahontas roads" in common parlance in railroad circles.

The N&W crossed fairly rugged terrain in movement of its heavy coal trains eastward from the coal fields, and began to develop very heavy and highly powerful steam locomotives around 1911, at about the same time that the same was occurring on C&O and the new Virginian. However, at this time the idea of electrification was gaining wide currency in railroad circles. N&W electrified its mainline between Iaeger, in the coal fields of West Virginia, and Bluefield, where the grades were steepest, in the period 1915-1925. This obviously influenced the development of steam motive power to some extent. It is worth noting that competing Virginian, also electrified an even longer stretch of its mainline out of the coal fields to Roanoke after 1925 when the economies of operation on the N&W

became evident. C&O stuck with steam exclusively, and the move for electrification stalled in the United States even while it was gaining momentum in Europe.

N&W and C&O campaigned in advertising to keep coal as America's foremost fuel, but after World War II the use of coal for domestic heating was quickly supplanted by oil, natural gas, and electricity, so coal began became almost strictly a fuel for industry (electric generation, other steam use, and metallurgical use), and the export trade grew exceptionally, first to rebuilding Europe and then to the world. N&W and C&O believed that they dared not shift to diesels with oil as fuel while preaching the use of coal, so they stuck doggedly to steam even as every other railroad went to diesels. Finally, in 1949, C&O got its first diesels and by the fall of 1956 was completely dieselized. The economies on many fronts were just to great to ignore.

Both C&O and N&W became involved in trying to perpetuate coal fuel for railroads by experimenting with a steam-turbine-electric design for locomotives, the C&O in 1948 and N&W in 1954. Both experiments failed. Both roads, along with other coal carriers also became involved in the research and development of a coal fired gas-turbine through the Bituminous Coal Research Institute. They believed that even if diesels were acquired, they would quickly pay for themselves and then could be replaced by the coal-fired gas turbines again. This was a dream unrealized.

N&W finally received its first diesels in 1955 and ran its last steam in 1960. Even at that it was the last to run mainline steam in America. In the later half of the 1950s N&W was the darling of the railfans and photographers as its huge steam locomotives made their treks across the landscape, and O. Winston Link's superb photos popularized the N&W far beyond the railfan community.

Unlike other railroads, N&W built all of its own new locomotives starting in 1927 at its massive Roanoke Shops. Its last commercially built engines were Y-3 class 2-8-8-2s from American Locomotive Company's Richmond Works and were among the last that plant produced before Alco closed it. N&W had been building many of its own locomotives since 1881 when it established the subsidiary Roanoke Machine Works, which later became its shops when the companies were merged in 1882, so it had plenty of experience. N&W built a total of 447 steam locomotives. No other American railroad did as many. Along with this came a great expertise on the design of locomotives for best performance and economy, the hallmarks of N&W's steam operations, and the envy of other railroads in the later years.

N&W, almost unique among railroads, concentrated on the most economical use, operation, maintenance, and especially servicing of its locomotives. In the last 20 years of steam, it established a servicing system that allowed steam locomotives to be serviced at terminals and made ready for additional use in a very shirt time. In 1951 the average turnaround for servicing was 3 hours and 47 minutes. This allowed a much higher availability rate than on any other steam railroad and approached that of diesels, leading *Trains* magazine's editor, David P. Morgan, to say in the 1950s that N&W had dieselized using steam.

H. C. Wyatt, N&W Assistant Superintendent of Motive Power, wrote the following in the May 28, 1951 issue of *Railway Age*:

". . . Our situation differs from most other railroads in two respects. First, we have available along our railroad, in almost unlimited quantities, the cheapest known fuel coal. It is coal of the finest quality for power generation. Second, when other railroads began to turn to other types of power, we already had in service a substantial number of modern coal-burning steam locomotives. The railroads on which the greatest number of steam locomotives were replaced by other types did not have fleets of steam power as reliable, efficient, or as modern as our J's, A's, or Y-6's.

Regardless of what you may have read or heard about the steam locomotive, you should not overlook its virtues. First of all, it is an extremely rugged and simple machine. It will better withstand abuse than any other type of locomotive in existence. It has the ability to develop maximum power quickly when needed. The best illustration of this quality is the locomotive boiler's ability to evaporate in a given time ten times as much water as the most efficient stationary steam plant boiler. . . .

In spite of the steam locomotive's virtues, however, we are not complacent over what we now have. The relatively low overall efficiency of the conventional steam locomotive is recognized. It is extremely difficult to visualize any substantial improvement in this efficiency, because of the heat units necessarily wasted in using water to convert heat units from the burning of fuel to the steam work units used against the locomotive pistons. . . .

In recognition of this situation, our railroad is now working with a group of three manufacturing concerns in the development of a coal-fired steam turbine locomotive with electric drive. . . ."

He is a little bit disingenuous because C&O, just a few miles from his headquarters in Roanoke, had a fleet of essentially new high capacity steam locomotives, built in the preceding ten years and many built in 1948, that it was in the process of replacing with diesels even as he wrote these words.

*The last of N&W triumvirate of power was the remarkable Class A simple articulated 2-6-6-4, of which 43 were built between 1936 and 1950. A "Super Power" locomotive of high pedigree and tremendous power and speed, these locomotives were at the pinnacle of modern steam. N&W used them well on fast freights and in areas of the mainline where their ability to develop high horsepower at speed was best possible. Here 1219 powers a coal train, a task not often assigned to these high-steppers. (Railroad Ave. Enterprises Collection)*

However, the economies of diesel operation over steam were so great that eventually N&W had to relent. Even though it was building its own steam, it relied on outside manufacturers for appliances needed for the locomotives, and when these sources of supply stopped production, there really was no alternative.

In one other important way N&W went against conventional motive power wisdom and the practice of all other major railroads, and that was it its continued use of compound articulated locomotives to the very end. In 1911 N&W acquired is first compound articulated locomotives, commonly called Mallets, after the Swiss inventor of the concept. In these locomotives two sets of cylinders and drivers sat under a single boiler which supplied steam to the back set at high pressure. After this steam was used to drive the back set of drivers, then it was exhausted not into the atmosphere, but was sent to the much larger forward cylinders, where it was used again to drive the front set of drivers and then was finally exhausted. The two sets of cylinders and drivers (called engines) were swiveled under the boiler, so that the actual driving wheel base was short enough to negotiate existing lines. The advantage of this type of locomotive was the short wheelbases, the increased power in a single locomotive unit, and the economical use of steam generated by a set amount of fuel. The Mallets became an immediate success in American railroading and were widely ad-

opted by railroads that had to handle especially heavy trains at relatively slow speeds, because these engines were not suited for high speed operation. But, after about 1925 the design lost favor. It was supplanted by the "simple articulated" design. This took the same configuration, but instead of using the steam twice, high-pressure steam was admitted to both sets of cylinders. This gave the locomotive much more power and allowed for larger drivers and thus higher speeds. Very few compound articulateds were built after this date--except by N&W. N&W used its Y-class series to continue developing, improving, innovating and researching the compound articulated design right up to the Y-6b class built by Roanoke Shops in 1952. The Y-classes became the backbone of N&W's coal hauling motive power fleet, and were used in virtually every capacity on the railway from mine runs to mainline coal trains, empties, and even fast freights. The railway's mechanical department and shops honed the design until they were able to get a very high degree of performance out of what was considered by everyone else as an outdated design.

In 1937, however, N&W opted for its famous A-class, a simple articulated 2-6-6-4 that was among the most capable steam locomotives ever built anywhere. The Class A was used on the areas of the road where the grades were lowest and maximum horsepower could developed at speed. They also saw use

*This simplified map shows the N&W System's 2,200 miles as it crosses Virginia, West Virginia, Ohio and North Carolina, with just a few branch line miles in Kentucky. (TLC Collection)*

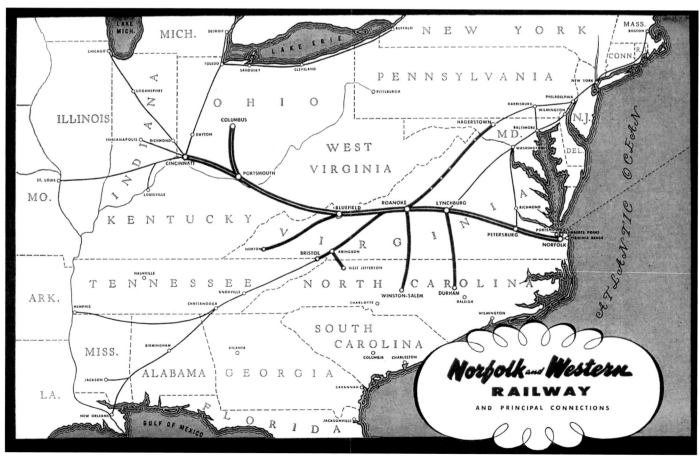

on the fast freights and some were even occasionally used in heavy passenger service. The A-class compares well with neighboring C&O's H-8 2-6-6-6 and the Union Pacific's much heralded 4-8-8-4 Big Boy. The efficacy of this design is argued convincingly in King's *Mercedes of Steam* book referenced earlier.

N&W's passenger trains were hauled first by the usual 4-4-0s and 4-6-0s, then when the 4-6-2 Pacific type and the 4-4-2 Atlantic type came into use, N&W adopted them as well. After C&O proved the value of the 4-8-2 Mountain type wheel arrangement in the mountains of Virginia and West Virginia just to the north of N&W, the latter adopted this design as well. But the ultimate design for passenger service was the much discussed J-class 4-8-4s.

The 4-8-4 came into use on the Northern Pacific in 1926, and very quickly gained wide acceptance both for passenger trains and for fast freight work. On the Pocahontas roads C&O adopted the type in 1935 for its mountainous territory between Charlottesville, Virginia, and Hinton, West Virginia. N&W probably studied the performance of these engines in that difficult terrain, and in 1940 built the first of its J-class. These locomotives had a bullet-nosed streamline design that has been acclaimed as one of the best attempts at streamlining a steam locomotive. But beyond their aesthetics, the Js were superb machines that rolled up more miles in service than their contemporaries, and regularly were assigned to runs that were longer than on most railroads, sometimes covering almost 500 miles without change at the head of one of the three N&W name trains, *The Powhatan Arrow*, *Pocahontas*, or *Cavalier*. Three more were added in 1950 to the first two groups, for a total of just 14 locomotives, yet they figure very prominently in the history of the 4-8-4 design.

N&W had few purpose-built switch engines, preferring to take older small locomotives such as a 2-8-0s and converting them to switching service. It was not until 1950, when N&W became interested in modern design switching locomotive, when it bought 30 essentially brand new 0-8-0s from C&O

when that road's sudden turn to diesels made them surplus. They were so well liked by N&W crews and mechanical men that the road built its own class of virtual duplicates, numbering 45 by 1953.

In 1954, when the future of steam seemed to be clouded even on N&W, the experimental steam-turbine-electric was tried. A single locomotive was built and given extensive testing, but by then the diesel was inevitable, and nothing would deny it. Therefore, as with C&O's turbine attempt in 1948, the N&W's design, though probably far better than C&O's, was shelved and the next year the first diesel appeared.

The next five years saw diesels and steam working on the trains that management thought best suited each type of motive power, and management still persisted in saying that steam would last into the future in the areas and in the service where it was best suited, only to completely surrender to the concept of complete dieselization in 1958, which was accomplished in late 1960.

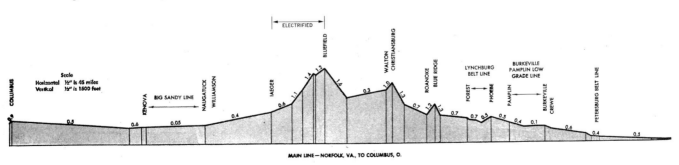

*N&W's profiles explain a great deal about its motive power. It had to bring coal east from West Virginia first across the Appalachian plateau near Bluefield, then over Alleghany Mountain at Christiansburg, and finally the Blue Ridge before heading downhill to the sea. Of course, the line from Iaeger to Bluefield was electrified.*

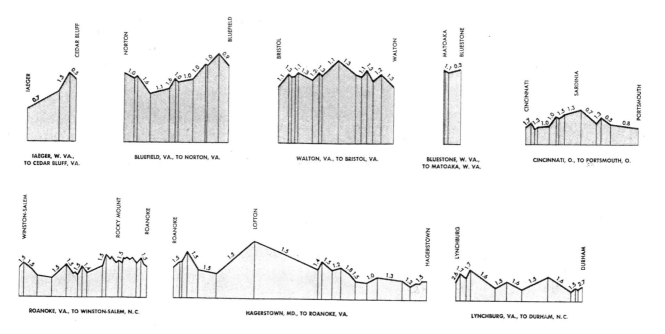

Profiles of N&W secondary lines are jagged in their own right, but none have the very long sustained grades that plagued the eastbound traffic out of West Virginia to the coast. Even the Portsmouth-Cincinnati line along southern Ohio had a saw-tooth profile. Nothing was easy for N&W motive power.

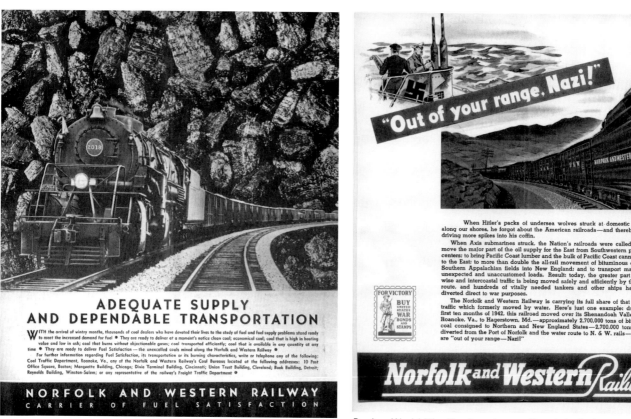

N&W had a superb public relations and advertising program that filled trade and national magazines, brochures, timetables, and newspapers with advertising not only about the line's passenger services, but about its freight trains and that greatest of all N&W commodities--coal. This ad appeared in the December 12, 1937 N&W passenger timetable, and featured Y-3 No. 2018 with a coal train while the sky was replaced by close-up of coal lumps. Pretty unusual for a passenger timetable. (TLC Collection)

During World War II railroads usually printed what are now very evocative ads, and N&W's usually juxtaposed its transportation system and machinery against German and Japanese soldiers and war machines. In this November 1942 ad N&W uses a Y-6a rushing along with coal and oil for the war effort and told the story of how its trains helped substitute for coastwise shipping as the U-boat packs prowled the east coast of the United States. The Y-class locomotives most often appear in N&W freight ads, and of course the J-class is in all the passenger material. (TLC Collection)

# 2: Z Class – 2-6-6-2s

## Beginnings of N&W's Modern Locomotive Fleet

This chapter is devoted to the Z-classes of 2-6-6-2 compound articulated locomotives which started N&W on its modern locomotive program in 1912. These locomotives set the stage for the development of the Y-classes of 2-8-8-2 compounds on N&W.

Until this time, N&W relied on the usual assortment standard steam locomotives for its freight business, including the 2-8-0, which was the most popular of all American locomotive wheel arrangements nationwide. It also had a rather peculiar attachment to the 4-8-0 which very few other railroads used at all.

In 1903 the Mallet compound articulated design came to American shores. The first of the type, an experimental 0-6-6-0, was built for the Baltimore & Ohio, which was looking for something with more power for carrying its increasingly heavy coal traffic over its several steep grades in northern West Virginia, Maryland, and through Pennsylvania. The idea of a compound locomotive was well known and had been used on a number of cross-compound non-articulated locomotives of the 2-8-0 type by several railroads. However, the idea of the articulated design with two engines under the same boiler, the second using the exhaust steam from the first, was new.

The design had been improved by 1909 so that 2-8-8-2s were built for the Southern Pacific which used them with success. The addition of the leading truck was found to be needed for any road engine and the trailing truck allowed for better support of the firebox and cab. In 1909 the new Virginian Railway decided to buy 2-6-6-0 Mallets, and in 1910 the C&O bought the first of its many 2-6-6-2s. That same year the N&W purchased two different types of compound articulateds: the X-1 class 0-8-8-0 and the Y-1 class 2-8-8-2, acquiring five of each from Baldwin Locomotive Works. The X-1 types were found inadequate because of their failure to have the lead and trailing trucks as well as other problems. The Y-1 2-8-8-2s were not entirely as successful as N&W wanted.

N&W then borrowed C&O 2-6-6-2 No. 773 from that line and tested it against the non-articulated and articulated designs in the N&W fleet in 1911, discovering that the C&O design could outperform anything that N&W had. The C&O 2-6-6-2 had a weight similar to the N&W 2-8-8-2s but had a superheater and a larger capacity boiler and was more powerful. As a result of the tests, N&W bought 2-6-6-2s that were close copies of the C&O locomotives in 1912 and within two years had 80 on hand. An additional 110 were received between 1914 and 1918.

Able to do the work of two or more 4-8-0s in the mountain territory, they were an immediate success, taking twice the loads over the grade at Elkhorn Tunnel. In all accounts the 2-6-6-2s were perfectly suited to N&W's terrain and traffic. C&O found the same to be true and purchased even larger quantities of the design for its mainline coal and merchandise trains, even though it had far easier grades than N&W. Classed Z-1 and Z-2, the 2-6-6-2s ruled the N&W mainlines until enough of the improved 2-8-8-2s were on hand to start replacing them in the heaviest work.

The Z-1 2-6-6-2s gradually assumed the duties that they would have in the period of this book's treatment (after 1930), handling some yard work, on local trains, and in mine run service supplying and picking up cars at the many branches that N&W soon had throughout the coal fields region.

Improvements included boiler pressure increase to 225 pounds (so tractive effort went to 90,996 in simple and 75,830 compound). Cylinders were changed from slide valves to piston values, and larger tenders were assigned, most of this "modernization" having been done by the early 1930s. After delivery of the first 15 locomotives (1300-1314) from Richnond in 1912, subsequent, improved locomotives were classed Z-1a. As they were rebuilt and modernized the Z-1a's were classed Z-1b. Z-1s were retired in 1934 and never rebuilt. Of the 175 Z-1a's, a total of 74 were rebuilt to Z-b by May, 1931. As of January, 1944, the N&W roster showed 50 Z-1a and 63 Z-1b locomotives.

The new fleet of 2-6-6-2s were aptly suited to this work with their short rigid wheelbase allowing them to travel on tight curves and axle loadings that allowed them on bridges that were not as strong as on the mainline. The fleet continued in this work with over 50 surviving into the last few years of steam, all being retired by 1958. In the post-1930 era these strong and versatile locomotives could be found in various work all over the system, but tended to concentrate in the coal fields and on the easier grade line east of Roanoke, as well as in heavy switching work, including hump yards.

A single class Z-2 locomotive was created in 1928 when No. 1399 was rebuilt as a simple locomotive. N&W was well aware that the compound locomotive was losing favor on most railroads, which were turning to simple articulated designs or the just developed "Super Power" design with the large free steaming boilers and larger firebox. Neighbor C&O had opted for its H-7 class simple 2-8-8-2s in 1924-26. These monstrous locomotives swept C&O's compound 2-6-6-2 off most mainline heavy trains immediately. Other railroads, including Union Pacific, Great Northern, and Southern Pacific as well as B&O were also converting older compounds to simple engines with varying success. It is not hard to imagine that N&W wanted to look into the simple articulated locomotive, therefore No. 1399 was rebuilt with four 22x32 inch cylinders and given extensive tests. However, its boiler was not able to supply sufficient high pressure steam to all four cylinders and it was ultimately scrapped in 1934. According to several N&W motive power historians, it yielded important lessons as N&W designed its highly successful A-Class 2-6-6-4 simple articulated locomotive which arrived in 1936.

The C&O also converted one of its H-4 2-6-6-2s, No. 1470, which was very similar to the N&W's Z-1a, to simple operation in 1928, concurrent with N&W's experimentation. It did not meet expectations, but was kept in service until 1947 as a one-engine class. The two roads shared the test data. On N&W it led to the Class A in 1936, on C&O to the H-8 2-6-6-6 in 1941.

## Summary Roster:

| | | | |
|---|---|---|---|
| 1300-1314 | (Z-1) | Alco-Richmond | 1912* |
| 1315-1379 | (Z-1a) | Alco-Richmond | 1913 |
| 1380-1419 | (Z-1a) | Baldwin | 1914 |
| 1420-1430 | (Z-1a) | Alco-Schenectady | 1915 |
| 1431-1459 | (Z-1a) | Alco-Schenectady | 1916 |
| 1460-1469 | (Z-1a) | Alco-Schenectady | 1917 |
| 1470-1489 | (Z-1a) | Alco-Schenectady | 1918 |

* All Z-1 class locomotive retired as a class in December 1934.

Numerous Z-1a locomotive rebuilt to Z-1b between 1928 and 1930. Z-1b rebuilds included: New style piston valve and steam chests; modern pilot and headlight; Worthington BL Feedwater Heaters; and larger tenders.

## Specifications - Z1a

### Weights:
| | |
|---|---|
| Lead Truck: | 23,000 lbs. |
| Drivers: | 354,500 lbs. |
| Trailer: | 49,500 lbs |
| Total Engine | 427,000 lbs. |
| Tender: | Various |

### Wheels:
| | |
|---|---|
| Leading Truck: | 30 inches |
| Drivers: | 56½ inches |
| Trailer: | 44 inches |
| | |
| Cylinders: | 35x32 inches |
| Boiler Pressure: | 225 pounds per square inch |

### Heating Surface:
| | |
|---|---|
| Flues: | 4,238 sq. ft. |
| Firebox: | 369 sq. ft. |
| Arch Tubes: | 22 sq. ft. |
| Superheater: | 971 sq. ft. |
| Total | 5,600 sq. ft. |
| | |
| Grate Area: | 72.2 sq. ft. |
| Firebox Inside: | 96⅛ x 108⅛ inches |
| Superheater: | Schmidt Type A |
| Stoker: | Street |
| | |
| Tractive Effort (Compound): | 75,830 lbs. |
| (Simple): | 90,996 lbs. |

*The official N&W mechanical diagrams on this and the following pages show the various configurations of the Z-1, Z-1a and Z-1b 2-6-6-2s with varying tenders and other modifications. (TLC Collection)*

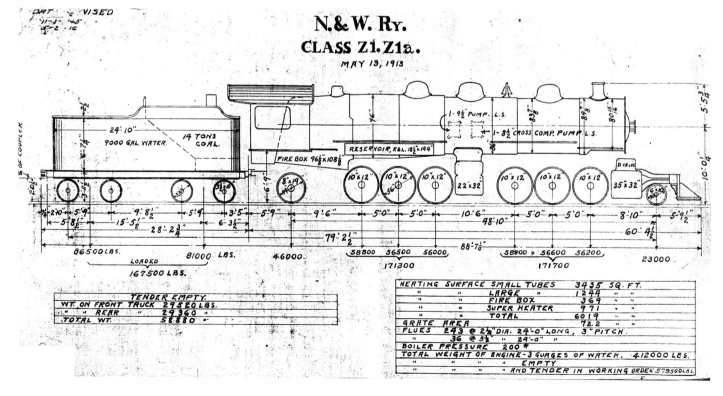

*Alco's builder portrait of Z-1 No. 1427, new at Schenectady in 1915 shows well its lines which comport very closely with the C&O's 2-6-6-2s. The small tender was, for some reason, characteristic of these locomotives on a number of railroads, and they were later replaced by ones with a much larger capacity for both coal and water. (Alco Photo, TLC Collection)*

*Z-1a No. 1317, built by Alco's Schenectady works in 1912 is shown in right ¾ profile at Columbus on July 28, 1933, early in the period we are studying, but over 20 years into the life of the locomotive. It has that 1920s-30s look with the small road name under the number on the cab, the large pilot-mounted headlight and high mounted number boards. A nice, clean looking "big engine" of the day, probably being used for coal train work between Columbus and Portsmouth. It was retired in 1944. (Robert Graham photo, Jay Williams Collection.)*

*This 1930s photo of No. 1362 shows the left side of the class in the 1930s era while still sporting the small tender. Location is not known. (TLC Collection)*

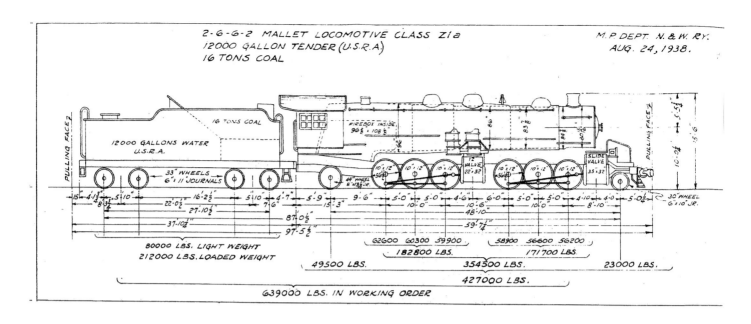

2-6-6-2 MALLET LOCOMOTIVE CLASS Z1a
12000 GALLON TENDER (U.S.R.A.)
16 TONS COAL

M.P. DEPT. N.&W. RY.
AUG. 24, 1938.

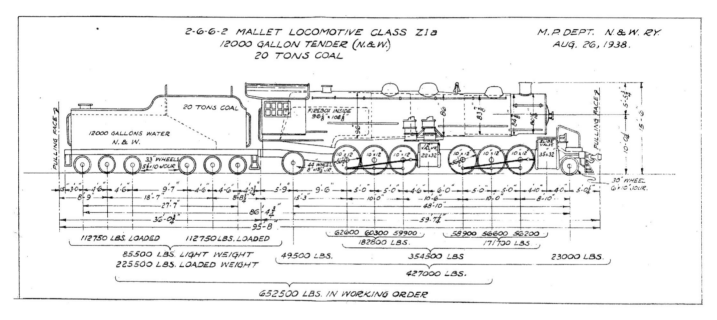

2-6-6-2 MALLET LOCOMOTIVE CLASS Z1a
12000 GALLON TENDER (N.&W.)
20 TONS COAL

M.P. DEPT. N.&W. RY.
AUG. 26, 1938.

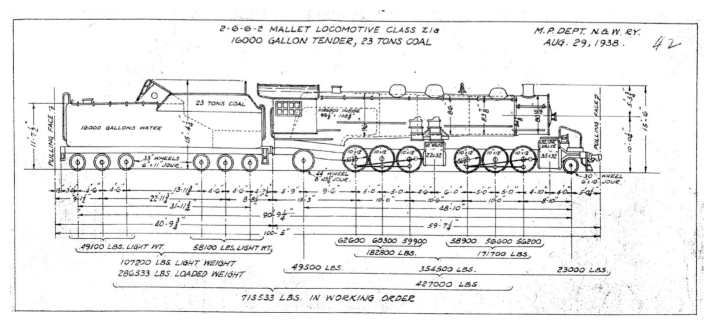

2-6-6-2 MALLET LOCOMOTIVE CLASS Z1a
16000 GALLON TENDER, 23 TONS COAL

M.P. DEPT. N.&W. RY.
AUG. 29, 1938.

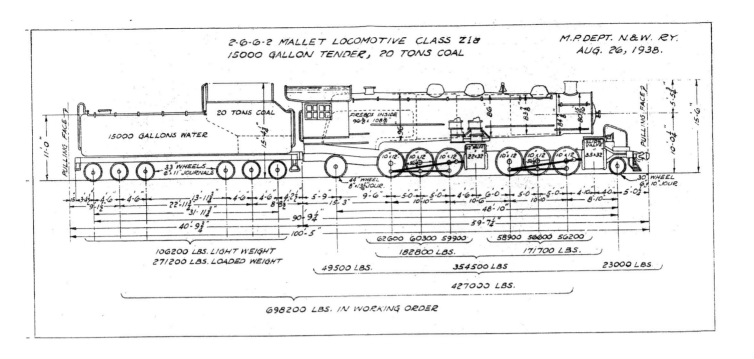

2·6·6·2 MALLET LOCOMOTIVE CLASS Z1a
15000 GALLON TENDER, 20 TONS COAL

M.P. DEPT. N.& W. RY.
AUG. 26, 1938.

20 TONS COAL

15000 GALLONS WATER

FIREBOX INSIDE
96⅛ x 108¾

33 WHEELS
6" x 11" JOURNALS

44 WHEEL
8" x 13½"JOUR.

30 WHEEL
G.F. 10"JOUR.

62600 60300 59900    58900 56600 56200

182800 LBS.    171700 LBS.

106200 LBS. LIGHT WEIGHT
271200 LBS. LOADED WEIGHT

49500 LBS.    354500 LBS.    23000 LBS.

427000 LBS.

698200 LBS. IN WORKING ORDER

---

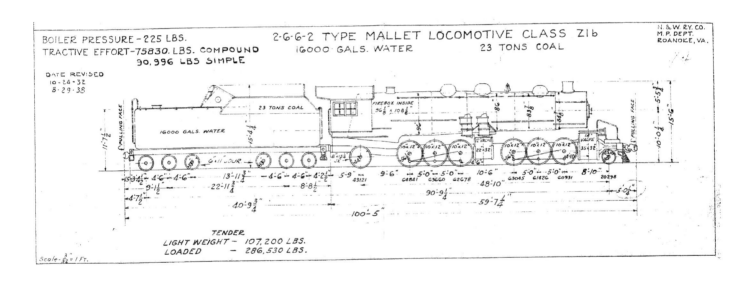

BOILER PRESSURE – 225 LBS.
TRACTIVE EFFORT–75830. LBS. COMPOUND
90,996 LBS SIMPLE

2·6·6·2 TYPE MALLET LOCOMOTIVE CLASS Z1b
16000 GALS. WATER          23 TONS COAL

N.& W. RY. CO.
M.P. DEPT.
ROANOKE, VA.

DATE REVISED
10-24-32
8-29-38

23 TONS COAL

16000 GALS. WATER

FIREBOX INSIDE
96⅛ x 108¾

6"x11" JOUR.

TENDER
LIGHT WEIGHT – 107,200 LBS.
LOADED      – 286,530 LBS.

Scale-³⁄₃₂"=1 Ft.

---

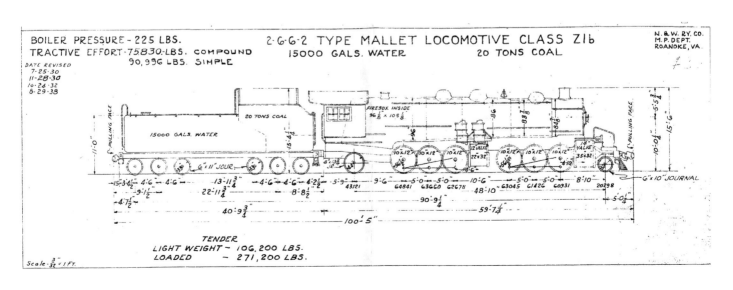

BOILER PRESSURE – 225 LBS.
TRACTIVE EFFORT–75830·LBS. COMPOUND
90,996 LBS. SIMPLE

2·6·6·2 TYPE MALLET LOCOMOTIVE CLASS Z1b
15000 GALS. WATER          20 TONS COAL

N.& W. RY. CO.
M.P. DEPT.
ROANOKE, VA.

DATE REVISED
7-25-30
11-28-30
10-24-32
8-29-38

20 TONS COAL

15000 GALS. WATER

FIREBOX INSIDE
96⅛ x 108⅝

6"x11" JOUR.

6"x10" JOURNAL

TENDER
LIGHT WEIGHT – 106,200 LBS.
LOADED      – 271,200 LBS.

Scale-³⁄₃₂"=1 Ft.

15

No. 1467 at Roanoke in 1931 has the larger tender but still has the low-pressure cylinder slide valves. (TLC Collection)

This photo shows No. 1341 at Roanoke on January 24, 1935, with improvements visible in the form of piston valves on the low-pressure cylinders. It also has the larger tender. (TLC Collection)

No. 1442 has new piston valves, large tender, and additional piping in this August 9, 1935 photo at Buena Vista on the Shenandoah Valley line. It still has the boiler-tube pilot. Most of these locomotives received a plain foot-board pilot in later years. (TLC Collection).

No. 1446 is getting fuel for its next trip (note fireman with shovel leveling out tender heap) in front of the old wooden coaling station at Roanoke. It has all the modernizations except for the pilot, and looks like it could have been taken in 1950, though the scene is from September 1, 1930. This locomotive was finally retired in November 1957, after just over 40 years of service. (William Monypeny, TLC Collection)

No. 1425 is at Norfolk at the late date of July 21, 1948, and looks like it has just been shopped or painted. It still has the slide values up front, having escaped that modernization, but has the footboard pilot and the large tender. It still has that 1920s look with the plain face, though by this time the number boards have been dropped from the top of the smoke box to beside the smaller headlight on the pilot deck. (TLC Collection)

Fully modern looking, No. 1442 is at Island Yard, Lynchburg, Virginia, in April 1950. Built in 1916, it had been on the road for 34 years and has received a great deal of attention over those years from the shops. (TLC Collection)

For comparison in appearance, here are 1467 (Norfolk, Aug. 29, 1948), and 1478 (Bluefield, Sept. 5, 1949). Both are among the last survivors of the class, yet have a decidedly different appearance. No. 1467 has the older look with the slide valves, yet has the foot-board pilot, while 1478 has a much newer look with the piston valves, and air pumps under the running board, but still has the boiler tube pilot. It somehow looks much more akin to N&W's modern power than does the 1467. (Both photos, TLC Collection)

No. 1352 has a coal train or at least a cut of loaded hoppers at Bluefield yard, while a Y-class brings a freight into the yard in the distance. (TLC Collection)

No. 1440 has a second section of the local freight in tow near Petersburg, Virginia, July 5, 1947, in this nice action scene. (H. Reid photo, TLC Collection)

*Left and Below: This summer 1954 set of photos shows Z-1b No. 1462 with caboose doing some local switching at Blue Ridge, Virginia. (John Krause Photo)*

*Working on the "Pea Vine" line (between Portsmouth and Cincinnati) Z-1a No. 1321, is at Clare Yard in Cincinnati on September 25, 1938. (Robert J. Foster Photo, TLC Collection)*

No. 1457, with white flags, is power for a mine run bringing in coal from the Dry Fork Branch to Iaeger in 1941. (L. D. Lewis Collection)

The lone Z-2 class 2-6-6-2, No. 1399 is seen here after it was rebuilt at Roanoke in 1928 as a simple locomotive. The cylinders and, of course, the prominent double exhaust stack mark this as different from its compound sisters. The slim boiler simply could not supply enough high-pressure steam for all four cylinders and the experiment was not successful, yet it yielded valuable test data that was used to develop the fabulous A-class simple articulated of 1936. The 1399 was retired and scraped in 1934. (N&W Photo, TLC Collection)

# 3: Y Class – 2-8-8-2s

## Workhorses of the N&W

N&W possessed more 2-8-8-2s than any other wheel arrangement in the era of this book's coverage. Its mechanical department improved and used them in a way like no other railroad in the United States. Indeed, the compound articulated design became the hallmark of the N&W in the last decades of steam, exemplified by the 2-8-8-2.

As discussed before, the compound articulated, or "Mallet" type steam locomotive first appeared in the U. S. in 1904 as a B&O engine. It soon gained wide acceptance during an era when the demand to haul ever-increasing loads at relatively slow speeds was the standard--known as the "drag era." It was only after World War I that the need for increased speed became more important to railroad managements, so that increasing numbers of trains could be dispatched over a given stretch of railway. Efficiency and its corollary, speed, became the bywords.

The 1920s was the high point of steam locomotive development. At the same time, it was the period of the diesel locomotive's early advancement. The diesel's coming-of-age took place in the last half of the 1930s, as the flashy, new lightweight streamliner passenger trains were usually hauled by diesels. Diesel road freight engines and yard switchers began to make noticeable inroads into the steam railroads' motive power fleets at the same time.

The watershed event in steam locomotive improvement likely came when Lima Locomotive Works, of Lima, Ohio, introduced a new concept called "Super Power" in 1924. It was simply a locomotive with a large furnace and boiler that could supply high-pressure steam at a steady rate, no matter what the conditions of operation. The engine's main characteristic was a large boiler and a large firebox supported by a four-wheel trailing truck. This set-up offered an unfailing supply of high-pressure steam under all operating conditions. Baldwin Locomotive Works and American Locomotive Company, the two other large builders, soon adopted Lima's concept. Most of the engines they constructed after the 1920s were along the Super Power design, though that particular name was a trademark of Lima (who built 699 such locomotives between 1924 and 1948).

Even before the Lima designs gained acceptance, several railroads were experimenting with the construction of simple articulated designs, or in converting compound articulateds to simple machines. "Simple" means that all four cylinders are supplied with high-pressure steam directly from the boiler, rather than the compound type that reused the steam.

In compound types, the high-pressure went to the rear cylinders and then once used for mechanical power there, trav-

elled to the much-larger, low-pressure cylinders of the front engine. There it expanded again, creating additional mechanical force before being exhausted.

In the simple design, high-pressure steam went to all four cylinders and, once expanded, was exhausted into the atmosphere. The first experimental simple articulated design was built as a single locomotive for the Pennsylvania Railroad, but not repeated.

In 1924-1925, the C&O, N&W's neighbor and sometime-competitor for coal traffic both east and west, decided to not just experiment with a simple articulated design, but to go all the way. The company ordered – from Alco in 1924 then Baldwin in 1926 – a total of 50 simple 2-8-8-2s. This was the first large order and operational use of simple articulateds on American railroads. The H-7 class, as the new engines were designated, was highly successful in both the C&O's coal traffic and fast freight. It increased tonnage capability and speed, and rendered the smaller 2-6-6-2 compounds obsolete.

The Virginian Railway, N&W's other competitor for eastbound coal traffic, also started its own articulated locomotive construction, in the 1909-1912 time period. Virginian first built 2-6-6-0s, but then added 2-8-8-2s to the fleet in 1910. Following were more of the type in the 1912-1919 period. Virginian never had a fleet of 2-6-6-2s, as did N&W and C&O. In 1916 it experimented with the ungainly 2-8-8-8-4 with a single unsuccessful locomotive. Then came the monstrous 2-10-10-2 in 1918, of which 10 were built.

Like N&W, Virginian electrified an important section of its mainline out of West Virginia to Roanoke, where the heaviest traffic was concentrated over the steepest grades. Virginian, however, just wasn't in the same league as N&W and C&O when it came to locomotive design and development. The line certainly startled the railroad world with the ungainly 2-8-8-8-2 and the small fleet of 2-10-10-2s.

N&W, ever mindful of what was happening in the steam locomotive development sphere, must have looked at C&O's simple H-7 2-8-8-2s and considered how it might use the simple articulated. It and C&O both (in 1928) tried experiments to convert 2-6-6-2s to simple operation (see Chapter 2, page 14) without success.

At this point, N&W had already stabled no less than 121 compound 2-8-8-2s in Y-1 through Y-5 classes. These locomotives were shouldering the bulk of the mainline coal and freight business, and most were relatively new. N&W also had pioneered development of these locomotives, and during the USRA period in World War I and following, its mechanical

NOTE: For a complete history of the Y-Class 2-8-8-2s, consult Norfolk & Western Y-Class 2-8-8-2 Articulated Steam Locomotive by Thomas W, Dixon, Jr., Karen Parker and Gene Huddleston, TLC Publishing, 2009

officials were key players in the USRA's design of the U. S. standard compound 2-8-8-2.

It can be inferred that since N&W had invested so much effort in the design and improvement of the compound design, plus building over 100 of these massive machines, the railroad was not anxious to precipitously jump into the simple articulated design work. Its management was much more cautious than C&O, even though N&W mechanical experts knew of C&O's success with its H-7 simple 2-8-8-2s. Rather, N&W kept on building 2-8-8-2s, with 10 more of them in 1927; 19 in 1930; and 11 in 1931, when the Depression stopped locomotive construction nearly everywhere.

All the while, the Lima Super Power concept was taking root, and a good number of single coupled and articulated designs were built for several major railroads before the Depression. This included Texas & Pacific's pioneer 2-10-4s of 1925, and C&O's massive T-1-class 2-10-4s in 1930. This was probably the quintessential Super Power engine, both in looks and performance.

By 1936, rail traffic was picking up. Since N&W experienced no great financial difficulty during the Depression years, it was ready for growth. The road planned a two-pronged approach to acquiring new freight power. First, Y-class 2-8-8-2 construction continued, right up to the end of steam operations. Secondly, the new 2-6-6-4 A-class simple articulated Super Power design was installed, and these engines were also built until steam's demise, though in smaller quantities than the 2-8-8-2s.

The new A-class was intended primarily for faster service on generally lower grades, where its full potential for horsepower development at speed could be realized. It was also used in general service.

In 1936-1937, 10 of the 2-6-6-4s were placed in service. After that, none were built until wartime traffic demanded not only more motive power, but additional speed and efficiency. Twenty more A's were built during the war. Following were eight more in 1949-1950, during N&W's last gasp at holding on to steam for the long term (see Chapter 4).

Here is the construction record for Y's and A's for the balance of the steam era (all built at N&W's Roanoke Shops):

|  | 2-8-8-2s | 2-6-6-4s |
|---|---|---|
| 1936 | 5 | 2 |
| 1937 | 2 | 8 |
| 1938 | 8 | - |
| 1939 | 9 | - |
| 1940 | 11 | - |
| 1942 | 16 | - |
| 1943 | - | 10 |
| 1944 | - | 10 |
| 1948 | 1 | - |
| 1949 | 7 | 5 |
| 1950 | 6 | 3 |
| 1951 | 3 | - |
| 1952 | 4 | - |

Though the early Y-1s were moderately successful, the later

William E. Warden, an N&W steam aficionado, wrote the following about N&W's 2-8-8-2s:

In the steam days, every railroad had its workhorses. These were the versatile locomotives that could handle just about any job on the line. Originally designed for "drag freight" service, where speed was sacrificed for tonnage, the N&W 2-8-8-2 Y-class Mallets soon got the workhorse name as they were often used in hump yard and switching service as well as fast freight, locals, and as pushers. They could meander up branch lines with locals and mine runs, help push 100-car coal drags up tortuous grades, or muscle work trains out on the mainline.

Most of N&W's Mallets had a provision for "jump starting" wherein high pressure boiler steam could be fed through a reducing valve directly into the low pressure cylinders during start-up. Thus, a Y-class could be operated "simple" at low speeds. This feature was generally cut off – by the engineer – at about 10 miles per hour.

Additionally, some of the Y's were built with an ar-

rangement giving the low pressure cylinders a shot of high pressure steam directly from the boiler whenever faster acceleration or extra tractive effort was needed. This feature was also added to many older Y's as they were overhauled at Roanoke Shops.

About the only place where the 2-8-8-2s couldn't make the grade, in a manner of speaking – at least for several decades – was in the vicinity of West Virginia's Elkhorn Tunnel, where a rise of 105 feet to the mile (a 1.8 percent grade), 13-degree curves, and poor tunnel ventilation, made navigating this piece of real estate hazardous to a engine crew's health. The tunnel, plus trackage between Bluefield and Vivian, was electrified in 1914. This electrification was later extended to Iaeger. A line relocation, including a new Elkhorn Tunnel with better ventilation, a 1.4 percent ruling grade, and greatly reduced curvature was opened in June 1950, allowing the elimination of the electrified territory, and allowing 2-8-8-2s finally to conquer every Appalachian hill on the N&W. This was one of the few times in history that steam ever replaced electric power on a railroad, and it was the last time.

classes, especially the Y-3s and Y-3a's in the years immediately following World War I, came into their own and set the pattern for N&W motive power until diesels conquered. It is notable that the last steam locomotives to operate on N&W were 2-8-8-2s.

The Y-6b class, N&W's ultimate compound articulated, was built 1948-1952 and accrued all the considerable art of steam design accumulated by the long experience and extensive experimentation done by N&W's nonpareil mechanical staff. In the early 1950s during a test run with the railway's trusty and well-used dynamometer car (a specially designed car used to test locomotive efficiency), showed a peak horsepower of about 5,500 at 25 mph, and above this speed the horsepower delivered to the train quickly decreased. By comparison, the 2-6-6-4 Class A simple locomotive developed a drawbar horse-power of 5,200, but this was not reached until it was operating at 35 mph. However, it was still at 5,000 when 60 mph was reached. Despite the improvements that were made over 40 years of building compound articulateds by N&W, it still was suited only to a certain service. The decision to supplement it with the A-class simple locomotive proved a sound one.

The 2-8-8-2 compound locomotives, of which N&W owned a total of 232 in Y-1 through Y-6b classes, the vast majority were still in operation at the end of steam. The Y-1s were the first to go, having been considered so relatively unsuccessful that they were all scrapped in 1924. But many of the Y-2s and Y-3s from 1918 were still in service into the late 1940s and early 1950s, a testament not only to N&W's quick learning curve in designing the compound articulated, but to the constant rebuilding, improving, and careful maintenance that was characteristic of N&W shops.

In the history of the American locomotives, there were approximately 700 2-8-8-2s built, of which about 600 were compound. N&W accounts for about half of that number. Alfred W. Bruce writing in *The Steam Locomotive in America* (1952) says: "These Norfolk & Western engines are probably the most highly developed articulated compounds ever built and give remarkable service on a road that operates them within their inherent limitations." There could hardly be a better summary of the Y-classes.

### 2-8-8-2s by Class

| Class | Road Number | Number of Locomotives | Dates Built |
|-------|-------------|-----------------------|-------------|
| Y-2 | 1700-1730 | 31 | 1918-1919 |
| Y-3 | 2000-2079 | 80 | 1919-1923 |
| Y-4 | 2080-2089 | 10 | 1927 |
| Y-5 | 2090-2119 | 30 | 1930-1931 |
| Y-6 | 2120-2154 | 35 | 1936-1940 |
| Y-6a | 2155-2170 | 16 | 1942 |
| Y-6b | 2171-2200 | 30 | 1948-1952 |

No attempt is being made to provide specifications for all classes, however, we have selected the Y-3 and the Y-6b to illustrate typical examples of the Y-classes:

### Specifications - Y-3

**Weights:**

| | |
|---|---|
| Lead Truck: | 34,640 lbs. |
| Drivers: | 548,500 lbs. |
| Trailer: | 28,300 lbs |
| Total Engine | 531,000 lbs. |
| Tender: | Various |

**Wheels:**

| | |
|---|---|
| Leading Truck: | 30 inches |
| Drivers: | 57 inches |
| Trailer: | 30 inches |
| Cylinders: | 39x32 inches |
| Boiler Pressure: | 240 & 270 pounds per square inch |

**Heating Surface:**

| | |
|---|---|
| Flues: | 5,300 sq. ft. |
| Firebox: | 388 sq. ft. |
| Arch Tubes: | 65 sq. ft. |
| Superheater: | 1,582 sq. ft. |
| Total | 7.335 sq. ft. |
| Grate Area: | 96.3 sq. ft. |
| Firebox Inside: | 8-ft.-¼ in. x 14 ft.-2-1/8 in. |
| Superheater: | Schmidt Type A |
| Stoker: | Duplex |
| Tractive Effort (Compound): | 101,470 lbs. |
| ( Simple): | 121,764 lbs. |

### Specifications - Y-6b

**Weights:**

| | |
|---|---|
| Lead Truck: | 34,640 lbs. |
| Drivers: | 548,500 lbs. |
| Trailer: | 28,300 lbs |
| Total Engine | 611,520 lbs. |
| Total Eng. & Tender: | 900,120 lbs. |

**Wheels:**

| | |
|---|---|
| Leading Truck: | 30 inches |
| Drivers: | 58 inches |
| Trailer: | 30 inches |
| Cylinders: | 39x32 inches |
| Boiler Pressure: | 300 pounds per square inch |

**Heating Surface:**

| | |
|---|---|
| Flues & Firebox: | 4,915 sq. ft. |
| Superheater: | 1,478 sq. ft. |
| Total | 6,393 sq. ft. |
| Grate Area: | 106.2 sq. ft. |
| Firebox Inside: | 8 ft.-10-¼ in. |
| Superheater: | Schmidt Type A |
| Stoker: | |
| Tractive Effort (Compound): | 126,838 lbs. |
| (Simple): | 152,206 lbs. |

## Wandering Y's

During the motive power-hungry years of World War II, several major railroads sold older motive power to other roads that needed it. N&W sold several of its Y-class 2-8-8-2s to other lines as follows:

| | |
|---|---|
| Bingham & Garfield RR | 2 Y-2s in 1943 |
| AT&SF | 8 Y-3s in 1943* |
| D&RGW | 15 Y-2s and Y-2a's in 1943 and 1945 |
| PRR | 6 Y-3s in 1943 |
| UP | 5 Y-3s in 1945 |

\* AT&SF sold 7 of the Y-3 third-hand to Virginian in 1947.

## The Y-2 Class

The first really successful 2-8-8-2 class on N&W, it set the stage for the USRA designs and the N&W's own Y-3

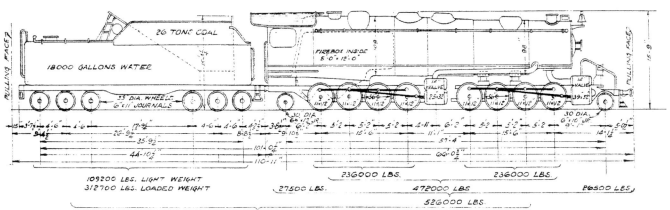

Y-2 No. 1701, built by Roanoke Shops in 1919, is shown here at Clare yard, in Cincinnati, in September 1937. By this time it had a large standard N&W tender replacing the small-capacity version with which it was first equipped. It was one of the locomotives that N&W sold to D&RGW in 1943, when that road need extra power. The smoke-box mounted air pumps with the horizontal oval door set this apart from most of the later Y-class engines in appearance. (H. K. Vollrath Collection)

Still in service at Roanoke in October 1949, No. 1716 (built by Roanoke in 1919) would finally retire in June 1951, along with No. 1704, the last working Y-2s. (H. K. Vollrath Collection)

## The Y-3 & Y-3a Classes:

The Y-3 class comprised 80 locomotives and was built during the high period of compound locomotive construction by American railroads. The locomotives of this class endured, with many modifications and improvements, to the end of steam. The exception are those sold during World War II. The class was intimately connected with the USRA design for the standard 2-8-8-2, in that N&W's own mechanical people were also on the USRA's design committee; not surprisingly the USRA design and the N&W's Y-3s were very much alike. The 80 locomotives in the Y-3 (and later Y-3a) class were the largest group of N&W 2-8-8-2s and came in a clump in the years immediately after World War I. They were indeed the backbone of the fleet during the most of the period, though eclipsed in mechanical sophistication by more refined designs in the later classes.

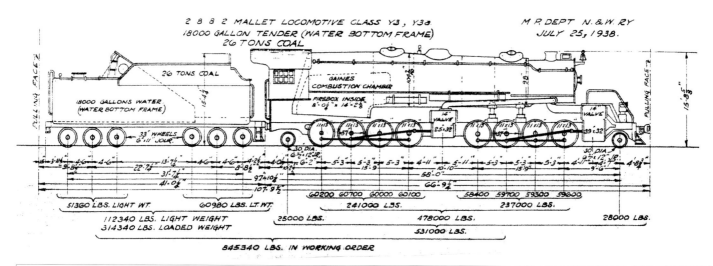

*Y-3 No. 2005 was among the first of the class, built by Alco's Schenectady Works in 1919. It had the flying pumps arrangement then popular on roads with big engines and small clearances. No. 2005 lasted to the very end in June 1958. (TLC Collection)*

*By the 1930s, the early Y-3 experienced modifications, improvements and appearance changes that made them look like this, a far cry from the way Alco delivered them in 1918. Here No. 2006 rests at Roanoke in the late 1930s. (TLC Collection)*

*Y-3 No. 2037 is creating a great show for the photographer in this October 14, 1938 view west of Roanoke. Most N&W coal trains flew the white flags of extra trains. (TLC Collection)*

*On a mine run on the main line in the coal fields, No. 2017 makes a good show of exhaust in the late 1940s. (Railroad Avenue Enterprises Collection)*

*The Y-3 is at Portsmouth, Ohio, in November 1958, a date which the eventual conquest of the diesel could be felt viscerally. This angle gives a particularly good appreciation of how the locomotive was put together and functioned. Modelers are always interested in how railway equipment looked from the top, and this photo helps somewhat. (Don Etter photo, Jay Williams Collection)*

*These two photos show Y-3s in their final appearance, right and left sides. The air pumps were located on the right side of the boiler, just opposite the feedwater heater on the other side. These locomotives are at Portsmouth in the 1950s. (Don Etter photos, Jay Williams Collection)*

Bluefield, West Virginia, was indeed a busy, smoky place in the days of N&W's steam operations. As the quarters of the Pocahontas Division, it was the hub of the coal fields. In this 1956 view, Y-3 No. 2040 pauses with other 2-8-8-2s, including Y-6a No. 2170. The ultra-modern engine terminal facility is seen in the background. These facilities were located at all N&W's major terminals and had the most modern steam servicing equipment available. They helped N&W use its modern steam so that turn-around times were comparable to contemporary diesels. A remnant of this facility is still in use in the form of the former "lubratorium," now the NS Bluefield shop. The imposing structure in the left background is the railroad YMCA. (Joe Schmitz photo, TLC Collection).

Y-3s, as well as other 2-8-8-2s, were often used for heavy switching. Here, at Portsmouth, No. 2009 is moving a heavy cut of loaded coal at the hump yard. As hump push-pullers, the 2-8-8-2s were ideal: power, traction, and slow speed operation. (Don Etter photo, Jay Williams Collection)

## The Y-4 Class

These 10 2-8-2-8s were delivered to N&W by Alco's Richmond Works. They were the last commercially built steam locomotives bought by N&W. From that point, all N&W motive power was built at Roanoke Shops. It is interesting to note, too, that these were the last big locomotives built at Richmond. It closed in September 1927 (after finishing Southern's Ps-4 4-6-2s).

As with the C&O, N&W liked to buy from Alco's Richmond Works so as to patronize the only locomotive builder below the Mason-Dixon Line. The Y-4s were numbered 2080-2089 and initially called "Y-3b" by the railway. They were very close copies of the Y-3/USRA design. These engines still had the archaic-looking spoked wheels on the engine and trailing truck, but came with the-then standard larger 23-ton/16,000 gallon tender (later upgraded to 26-tons/18,000 gallons). The boiler pressured was later raised to 270-psi. N&W then reclassified them as Y-4. Ultimately they received 27-ton/24,000-gallon tenders. These were acquired secondhand from Atlantic Coast Line in 1948.

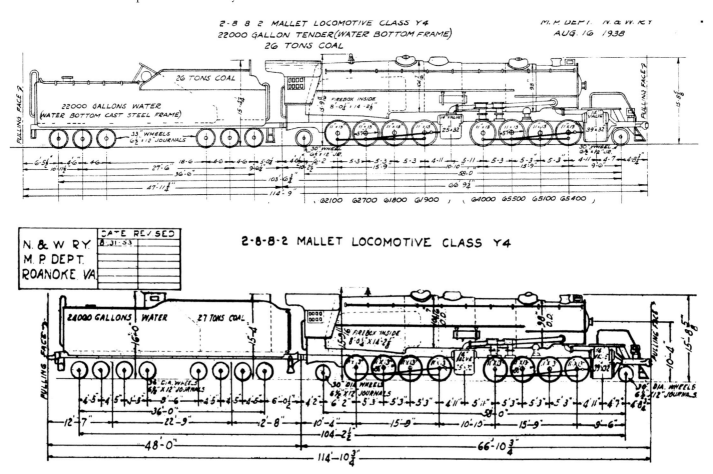

These diagrams show the Y-4 with two different tenders, including the massive 24,000 gallon eight-axle tender the N&W acquired second-hand from the Atlantic Coast Line railroad.

*Y-4 No. 2084 may be seen in left, ¾-profile at Shenandoah, Virginia, while working the Valley line on August 16, 1953. It has the giant ex-ACL tender, which sets it apart from other Y-class locomotives visually.*

*Again on the Shenandoah Valley line, No. 2080 is handling a fast freight train for which that line was noted. By the mid-1950s date of this photo, the locomotive has been modified with new front cylinders, valves, and bridge pipe. The latter looked like an inverted "V," or "wishbone," between the low-pressure cylinders out in front of the smoke box. This significantly improved steam flow from the big cylinders. It, too, has the large ACL tender characteristic of the class. (John Krause photo, TLC Collection)*

*When this photo was taken of Y-4 No. 2084 at Clare yard in Cincinnati, on September 28, 1938, it had not received many of the changes that would visually identify the class; no wishbone bridge pipe up front and no ACL tender. (TLC Collection)*

## The Y-5 Class

Numbered 2100-2119, these were the first of the Y-classes built by N&W at the Roanoke Shops in 1930-1932, just as the Great Depression was settling in and causing a steep decline in railroad traffic. Of course N&W, with its reliance on coal, was able to weather this financial storm well. The Y-5s were the first departure from the close adherence to the USRA standard. They boasted 300-psi boiler pressures, the highest yet for any of N&W's compound articulateds. They were also about eight tons heavier that the Y-4s. Their rated tractive effort was 126,838 lbs. compound, and 152,206 lbs. simple. Even though the cast frame had become more or less standard for new locomotives at the builders, N&W decided to use a built-up frame for the Y-5s. They had the inverted "V," or wishbone

exhaust pipes, in the front to facilitate the movement of steam from the low-pressure cylinders to the stack, thus decreasing back-pressure.

In service they were capable of hauling 5,000 tons from Bluefield to Roanoke without a helper, and 12,000-ton trains from Eckman to Williamson unassisted. East of Roanoke they were rated for 8,000 tons to Crewe, Virginia, unassisted over the Blue Ridge grade, or 9,000 tons with helper. These powerful engines were almost at once shopped and given improvements, and eventually were outfitted with cast steel frames, roller bearings and ballast that increased the engine's weight. The heating surface was also decreased on some locomotives during modifications in the 1930s-1940s, causing increased boiler efficiency. They became interchangeable with the newer Y-6s.

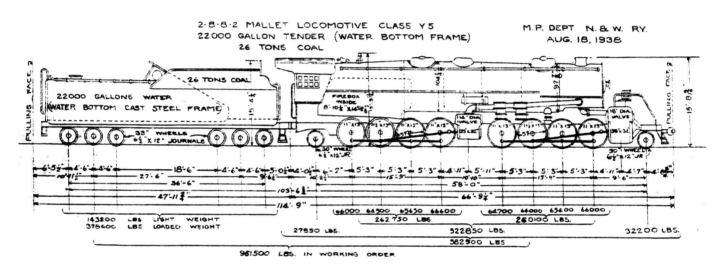

Y-5 No. 2114 is stopped as another train runs around it on the Christiansburg Grade (climbing Alleghany Mountain). This photo shows the new, large exhaust pipes that allowed better flow from the front cylinders to the exhaust nozzle. This "wishbone" shape gave the Y-5s an even more massive and powerful appearance. (Railroad Ave. Enterprises Collection)

No. 2109 takes coal at the huge coaling station at Portsmouth in the early 1950s. The Y-5s were often seen operating in the Ohio area. (TLC Collection)

At home in the coal fields as well, Y-5 No. 2015 is at the Iaeger, West Virginia, Terminal in the early 1950s. This shows the casing for the firebox lagging. The Y-5s were the first to have this feature. (Gene Huddleston photo, TLC Collection)

### The Y-6 Class

The Y-6s were built between September 1936 and November 1940, just in time to help N&W with its huge World War II freight load. Completed concurrently with the first of the new-concept A-class simple articulateds, which shared the erecting floor at Roanoke Shops, the Y-6s were the first of the truly "modern" compound articulateds. Indeed, they were the only new compound locomotives in American railroading at the time. Not seeking more power, N&W designers created an improved design emphasizing economy and ease of fabrication, decreased downtime for servicing and, most importantly, increasing fuel economy/efficiency to the degree possible for a reciprocating steam locomotive.

It was the beginning of the final chapter for the Mallet concept. They were built with cast steel beds with integral cylinders. All journals were equipped with roller bearings, and automatic lubricators (actuated by the valve gear) served cylinders, steam chests, guides, and 21 other moving parts. N&W claimed that the Y6s could best diesels when it came to line haul and servicing time. In tests, they could reach 4,200 horsepower at 25 mph, and travel 6,000 miles in active use per month.

These engines had 22-ton/26,000-gallon tenders, insuring they could travel from terminal to terminal without fuel/water problems. As with other Y-classes they were used on mainline freights and coal trains, and also as switchers, pushers, and mine run engines. They could take 14,500-ton trains from Iaeger or Welch to Williamson, West Virginia, and 13,000 tons on the Scioto Division to Columbus.

With a pusher helping over Blue Ridge grade, the Y-6s could handle 8,000 tons from Roanoke to Crewe. East of Crewe, they were limited to 125 cars. After WWII, they pulled 14,500-ton trains from Crewe to Norfolk.

In short, the Y-6s were the most versatile and efficient of the Y classes up to that point. The subsequent Y-6a subclass was essentially identical to the already excellent Y-6. The Y-6b, on the other hand, as described later in this chapter, was deservedly considered the pinnacle of N&W compound steam, and virtually all the Y-6s and Y-6as, as well as most of the Y-5s, were modified to match its excellent design.

*One of N&W's favorite spots for its publicity photos was near the Palisades of New River close by Pembroke, Virginia. This is the setting for this scene of Y-6 No. 2151 with a long train of uniform hopper cars, about 1947. (N&W Photo, Jay Williams Collection)*

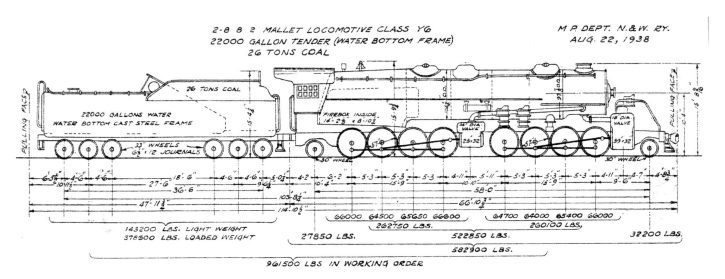

2-8 8 2 MALLET LOCOMOTIVE CLASS Y6
22000 GALLON TENDER (WATER BOTTOM FRAME)
26 TONS COAL

M.P. DEPT. N.&W. RY.
AUG. 22, 1938

Diagram of the Y-6. The later Y-6a was virtually identical, so this diagram can be considered to describe it as well.

N&W's various steep grades were a challenge to its locomotives. Part of the problem was improved by electrification, but on the Blue Ridge grade east of Roanoke, it was steam all the way. In these photos we see Y-6 No. 2140 and A-Class No. 1226 heading up an assault on Blue Ridge in 1956. In the second scene Y-6 No. 2140 is on the front with a pusher as helper (out of sight) this time. This particular view gives a good appreciation of the sloped top/sides of the tender coal bunker. (Both, Robert O. Hale photos, Jay Williams Collection)

*Class A 2-6-6-4 is the road engine on this Blue Ridge assault, with Y-6 No. 2152 assisting in front. Out of sight at the rear is another Y-class as the train nears the top of the grade. (TLC Collection)*

*Again on the Blue Ridge grade, Y-6 No. 2135, with auxiliary tender, leads a coal train along N&W's heavily-laid and well-maintained main line in June 1954. Scenes like this were the image of N&W in the later steam era. (John Krause photo, TLC Collection)*

*A nice overhead view shows the top of No. 2154 at Vickers, Virginia, ca. 1950. (Jay Williams Collection)*

Down on the Durham line, No. 2123 moves in the yard while a 4-8-2 sits with a work train to the left, at Durham, North Carolina, January 20, 1950. (H. Reid photo, TLC Collection)

The night watch at Iaeger, West Virginia, in the heart of the coal fields, finds No. 2154 ready for action, either on an early morning mine run, or to take a coal train east, about 1958. (William Gordon photo)

No. 2135 is powering manifest freight train No. 88 past the water tank at Luray, Virginia, on the heavily-trafficked Shenandoah Valley line May 1, 1954. (Jay Williams Collection)

The date is July 21, 1957, and Y-6 No. 2143 is pulling hard out of Christiansburg Tunnel. The "Christiansburg hill" was one of the operational snags for N&W as the line assaulted Alleghany Mountain. (Jay Williams Collection)

### The Y-6a Class

This class of 16 2-8-8-2s is distinguishable by sight only by looking at the numbers (2155-2170). When the need for power to meet war-time needs became evident, N&W built this class as virtual duplicates to the Y-6s, with which they were very pleased. The designation of Y-6a was because of minor differences, including an improved Worthington BL-2 feed water heater, and use of various materials other than steel for certain parts. This was because of the war-time need to conserve steel consumption. They had service lives that paralleled the Y-6 main class in every regard.

Y-6a No. 2166 rides the massive turntable at Shaffer's Crossing, Roanoke, in July 1956. (TLC Collection)

*No. 2163 with a second section manifest freight (green flags) east of Elliston, Virginia, May 10, 1954. (Jay Williams Collection).*

*No. 2167, with an auxiliary water tender, is pulling a empty hopper train between Christiansburg and Blacksburg in the summer of 1954. (John Krause photo, TLC Collection)*

*At home on the famous Blue Ridge grade, a Y-6a, such as No. 2166 here was used as both road power and pusher. This scene is from July 1956, as No. 2166 helps a fast manifest freight train over the grade. (TLC Collection)*

Out in the coal fields of West Virginia, Y-6a No. 2166 is ready for mine sifter work at Kermit in December 1958. (Gene Huddleston photo, Ron's Books Collection)

A snowy day in December 1958 sees Y-6a No. 2165 on a mine shifter run into Weller yard at Grundy, Virginia. The bridge is across the Levisa Fork of the Big Sandy River. The low-sided gondolas might be for a special movement, certainly not usual for a mine run. (Gene Huddleston Photo, TLC Collection)

## The Y-6b Class:

The final refinement of N&W's 2-8-8-2 came with the Y-6b class built between April 1948 and April 1952. The 30 locomotives in this class have received more than their fair share of attention over the years since the end of steam, possibly because they were the ultimate machines of their type.

After the end of World War II, N&W needed additional heavy power, mainly because of the new, steam-operated line in the area of Elkhorn Tunnel in West Virginia. The long-standing electric territory was completely eliminated, so more large locomotives were needed.

There were some important changes in the Y-6b, which included extension of combustion chamber from 42 to 84 inches. This permitted more complete combustion of gasses in the firebox before they entered the flues. The reducing valve was changed to manual so the engineer could shift to simple operation at any time. A "booster" valve was also fitted, allowing the engineer to add a small amount of superheated steam to the flow of exhaust steam feeding the low pressure cylin-

ders. These changes, taken together, were so successful that the 4,200 horsepower produced by the Y-6 and Y-6a, a considerable rating in its own right, was increased to a phenomenal 5,500 horsepower, and the increased tractive effort in the front engine required the addition of 13 tons of lead ballast to the frame to keep the engine from slipping. These changes were subsequently retrofitted to the earlier Y-6 and Y-6a classes and to most of the Y-5s as well.

The front end appearance was different because of the encasement of the Worthington SA feed water heater in the smoke box. This caused the front end to look odd, with a horizontal oval door. It was later rebuilt with a round door to make them look similar to other Y-classes. The air pumps were also rearranged, placing one on each side of the locomotive.

A Y-6b had the dubious distinction of being the last steam engine to operate on N&W - No. 2190's trip out of Williamson, West Virginia on May 6, 1960 was near the end. On September 30 of that year, N&W officially retired the last of its steam locomotives.

*Roanoke Shops' builder photo of the Y-6b shows one of that model built new with the round shoebox door. No. 2197 is the very locomotive that was pitted against EMD ABBA F-7 freight diesels when they were tested in 1954. N&W didn't buy the diesels--at least not then. (TLC Collection)*

*N&W's publicity department was in full cry when it issued this ad in September 1948, touting the new Y-6b, when no other steam was being built new for American railroads. (Trains Magazine, September 1948.)*

Showing the odd oval smoke box door, No. 2173 heads upgrade with Big Walker Mountain and the broad New River for background at Belspring, Virginia, in about 1949. (N&W Photo, TLC Collection)

This photo clearly shows the Y-6b in its original livery as No. 2185 poses at Bluefield on July 27, 1949. The reach rod for the front-end throttle and the original smoke box appearance are distinctive features. ( A. A. Thieme photo, TLC Collection)

Panned at speed, No. 2174 is on an empty hopper train assaulting Blue Ridge westbound near Villamont, Virginia, around 1956. (Robert Hale photo, Jay Williams Collection)

*Y-6b No. 2190 at the Iaeger coal dock in August 1957, is right in front of the new era - a GP9 EMD diesel. (W. G. Francher photo, Jay Williams Collection)*

*At the end of the new Elkhorn Tunnel, No. 2194 makes a grand exhaust show in the snow in January 1958. (William Gordon photo)*

*The ultimate in road freight power, the Y6b was also at home on mine runs up the coal branches. Here, No. 2176 backs with empties on the Dry Fork branch in 1958. (Gary Huddleston photo)*

*No. 2186 is making good time with coal near Ironton, Ohio, around 1950. (TLC Collection)*

# 4: A Class – 2-6-6-4s

## N&W's Simple Articulated

N&W built 43 simple 2-6-6-4 articulated locomotives between 1936 and 1950. They were most often used in fast freight service, especially in regions of the system where grades were relatively easy.

These engines had N&W road numbers 1200-1242. Only 65 2-6-6-4s were built in America, so N&W accounts for 66% of the type. The exact reason that N&W opted for this unusual wheel arrangement, instead a more common 4-6-6-4 arrangement, is not entirely clear. What is clear is that it built a superbly proportioned locomotive that was able to produce tractive effort and horsepower required for the service in which it was assigned.

Many steam historians look on the N&W Class A, as the 2-6-6-4s were designated, as a high point in steam locomotive development. It certainly was the last of such Super Power giants to be built. The last of class, No. 1242, was completed at Roanoke in 1950, at least two years after all other commercial steam locomotive construction had ended.

The A class formed one of the three legs in N&W's motive power plan, along with the Y class 2-8-8-2 compounds, and the J class 4-8-4s for passenger trains. In the years between the late 1930s and the end of steam in 1959-1960, these three types handled the majority of N&W trains and turned in the train-miles that made the line the envy of the railroads for its operating efficiency.

As mentioned earlier, neighbor C&O pioneered the production run simple articulated type in 1924-25 with 50 giant 2-8-8-2 simple locomotives. They were eminently successful in the service to which C&O assigned them. Both C&O and N&W participated in an experiment in 1928 in which each line converted a compound 2-6-6-2 to simple operation. In both cases the design was unsuccessful. However, it has long been suspected the Z-2 (as N&W's single simple 2-6-6-2 was classified), and the many tests by the line's dynamometer car, served as the basis for designing the Class A when economic conditions allowed.

Any plans for new locomotives were shelved during the Depression years and only in the mid-1930s did N&W think about the need for new motive power. Up to this time and for the prior decade, most of N&W fast freight trains were handled by K-3 class and K-1 class 4-8-2 Mountain locomotives, supplemented by some Y class 2-8-8-2s. This type was normally passenger power on most railroads. But several lines, such as N&W, used the Mountain type for both passenger and freight trains.

N&W's manifest freights ran between Norfolk and Colum-

bus or Cincinnati. These trains used the 4-8-2 on the Norfolk-Roanoke leg and Williamson-Columbus, with Y class 2-8-8-2s and the electrics handling many of them between, over the heavy grades of western Virginia and southern West Virginia.

Operationally, the K-1 4-8-2, normally a passenger engine, was a smooth rider and operated well at higher speeds, a natural outcome of its passenger pedigree. However, it lacked the power needed for a heavy freight train. The K-3s, which had better power production, were rough riding and very hard on track when running over 35 miles per hour because of heavy reciprocating parts. These conditions limited N&W's options for motive power and set the mechanical planners thinking about something that would out-perform the Mountain types and the compound 2-8-8-2 Y classes, particularly for faster operations. They decided on the A class with a wheel arrangement of 2-6-6-4. These were designed for operating at speeds up to 65 miles per hour, something simply not attainable for the 4-8-2s, nor for the ponderous 2-8-8-2s.

Since the coming of Super Power in the mid-1920s, N&W had not adopted the ideas embodied by this Lima Locomotive Works design. By the mid-1930s, the new concept gained adherents all over the country, and it was embraced by all three of the major commercial locomotive builders. The Super Power design provided a free-steaming boiler supplying sufficient amounts of high-pressure steam under all conditions and

## THOROUGHBREDS

THOROUGHBREDS of the turf and rail! On the well-graded, heavily ballasted Norfolk and Western Railway's roadbed—as well as on the race track—speed, endurance, power are the attributes of a thoroughbred ● Between the Midwest and the Virginias and Carolinas and between the North and the South, fast, powerful locomotives—thoroughbreds of the rails—haul merchandise freight trains on daily schedules comparable to those of passenger trains . . . providing safe, dependable, economical freight service—Precision Transportation.

**NORFOLK AND WESTERN RAILWAY**
PRECISION TRANSPORTATION
1838 — A CENTURY OF SERVICE — 1938

*This advertisement appeared in the July 15, 1938, N&W Public Timetable. Could it have been the inspiration for the NS's logos of today? The A's were ready to take the fast freights at racetrack speeds across the land. (TLC Collection)*

speeds. It almost always required a four-wheel trailing truck because of the inherent need for a very large firebox set entirely behind the drivers.

This did not go unnoticed in the mechanical department in Roanoke. Officials there carefully studied operations, not only on their own railway, but on others as well. They also had considerable test data available from the Z-2 and from the C&O's use of the 2-8-8-2 simple articulateds.

The planning and design work came together in 1935-36. In May and June 1936 the first two Class A 2-6-6-4s were constructed at Roanoke. No. 1200 was taken out for dynamometer car testing immediately after construction, and the results were reported in the September 26, 1936 issue of *Railway Age*. A few quotes from that article are presented here:

"Road tests which have been made with the new motive power indicate its ability to handle 4,800 tons on a 0.5 per cent grade at 25 m.p.h. On a comparatively level tangent this locomotive attained a speed of 64 m.p.h. with a 7,500-ton train. . . . It is interesting to note that the curve [horsepower and drawbar pull in pounds] shows drawbar horsepower. . . over 6,000 at speeds from 32 to 57 m.p.h., with a maximum of 6,300 at a speed of 45 m.p.h.

The boilers are of particular interest because of their size. With an overall length of 60 ft. 9-³/₁₆ in. and a light weight of 148,500 lb., they are longest and heaviest boilers that have been built to date for any N. & W. locomotives. The barrels are constructed in four courses ranging in diameter from 91 in. inside diameter at the first course to 105-½ in. outside diameter at the fourth course. The two front courses have 1-¹/₈-in. thick carbon steel sheets and the third and fourth courses have 1-in. and ¾ in. nickel steel.

The firebox is electrically welded throughout. The grate has a length of 13 ft. 10 in. and a width of 8 ft. 10-¼ in. with a grate area of 122 sq. ft. The combustion chamber is 9 ft. and 8 in. long. The boiler has 239 3-½ in. diameter superheater flues and 57 2-¼ in. diameter tubes. The length of the flues is 24 ft. 1 in. The construction of each boiler involved 2,970 rivets and 4,925 stay bolts. The boiler holds 8,100 gallons of water at the working height or 9,835 gallons when full. The boiler expands in length 1-⁵/₁₆ in. from cold to 330 lb. test pressure.

The boilers are designed for a working pressure of 300 lb. per sq. in. and safety valves are set at 275 lb."

Important dimensions were:

**Weights:**

| | |
|---|---|
| Lead Truck: | 30,300 lbs. |
| Drivers: | 430,100 lbs. |
| Trailer: | 109,600 lbs |
| Total Engine | 570,000 lbs. |
| Tender: | 378,600 lbs. |
| Total Eng. & Tender: | 948,600 lbs. |

**Wheels:**

| | |
|---|---|
| Leading Truck: | 36 inches |
| Drivers: | 70 inches |
| Trailer: | 44 inches |
| | |
| Cylinders: | 4x30 inches |
| Boiler Pressure: | 275 p.s.i. |

**Heating Surface:**

| | |
|---|---|
| Tubes & Flues: | 6,063 sq. ft. |
| Firebox & Comb. Chamber: | 530 sq. ft. |
| Arch Tubes: | 57 sq. ft. |
| Superheater: | 2,703 sq. ft. |
| Total | 9,353 sq. ft. |
| Grate Area: | 122 sq. ft. |
| | |
| Superheater: | Elesco Type E |
| Feedwater heater: | Worthington 6-s-A |

| Stoker: | Standard MB |
| --- | --- |
| Tractive Effort: | 104,500 lbs. |

**Tender:**

| | |
| --- | --- |
| Rectangular, | 26-tons/22,000 gallons |
| Tender Trucks: | 6-Wheel (Buckeye) on 1200 |
| | Commonwealth on 1201 |
| Bearings: | Timken Roller Bearings on all engine |
| | and tender axles. |

**Length:**

| | |
| --- | --- |
| Engine: | 72 ft. 7-¾ in. |
| Tender: | 47 ft. 11-¾ in. |
| Total | 120 ft. 7-½ in. |

**Wheel Bases:**

| | |
| --- | --- |
| Driving: | 35 ft. 5 in. |
| Rigid Driving: | 12 ft. 11-¾ in. |
| Total Eng. & Tender: | 108 ft. 7-¼ in. |

During the summer and fall of 1936, Nos. 1200 and 1201 were extensively tested and used in regular manifest freight train service with great success and pleasing results for the N&W mechanical department.

In 1937, eight more A class locomotive were built at Roanoke. They were enough to handle manifest freights operating between Norfolk and Roanoke, and between Williamson and Columbus. Y classes and the electrics handled these trains in the mountainous territory in between. K-3 class 4-8-2s continued to supplement the A Class locomotives when business required.

As their newest and best, No. 1206 was displayed by N&W as its contribution in the 1939-40 World's Fair in New York.

During World War II the existing 10 Class A locomotives were worked to their maximums, and N&W decided to build more for the expanding business: 15 in 1943 and 10 in 1944, with slight modifications from the original batch. No. 1210-1234 had working pressure increased to 300 psi, and an engine weight of 573,000 (up 3,000 pounds). They were rated at 114,000 lbs. tractive effort. Tenders were changed in size to hold 30 tons of coal and 20,000 gallons of water. These locomotives also were built with a lower crown sheet to prevent carryover of water when working hard, a design deficiency on the first group in service.

The Class A was equipped to handle passenger trains as they did before the war. During the conflict they were often used on heavy troop trains. An A class was also regularly assigned to SR-N&W trains 41 and 42 between Monroe and Bristol, up to the arrival of additional passenger power in the form of the first J class engines in 1941. They appeared leading other passenger trains as needed, when special or additional movements required, or exceptionally heavy trains were being operated. They had all the power that was needed and they had the speed.

Following the war, an additional five were built in 1948 and three more in 1950. They were assigned to help the additional freight burden transferred to steam operations when electrified territory was closed with the new line at Elkhorn. During the early 1950s, they, along with many Y classes locomotives, received auxiliary water tenders rebuilt from surplus standard N&W tenders.

Although regularly assigned to manifest freights, they seldom operated on the Shenandoah Valley line. When necessary, they handled coal trains and empties on the mainline over the mountains.

In appearance, the A class is compact and powerful-looking.

*No. 1223 is moving manifest train No. 92 at a good speed along the tangent track near Myrtle, Virginia, on the line between Petersburg and Norfolk about 1950. This is as clean a stack as any motive power official could want. (H. Reid photo, TLC Collection)*

It is also fairly clean with its large firebox lagged and jacketed. Most had a solid pilot with retractable coupler developed for the J class in 1941. This gave them a distinctive look, different from other N&W articulateds. Not all had this appearance throughout their lives: pre-war A's had the boiler-tube pilot, and those built starting with 1212 had the solid pilot. However, most of the earlier locomotives were retrofitted with this configuration. The solid pilot definitely added to the good looks of the class.

The A class has been widely discussed as to its relative efficiency in steam utilization and mechanical applications, and compares well with most other large simple articulated types. No. 1218 was saved from scrap and used as a stationary steam generator at a power plant. It was bought back by N&W and used in the 1980s to power excursion trains on the Norfolk Southern system before retirement to the Virginia Museum of Transportation, where is sits today.

*Mechanical erection drawings for N&W Class A. (Railway Age)*

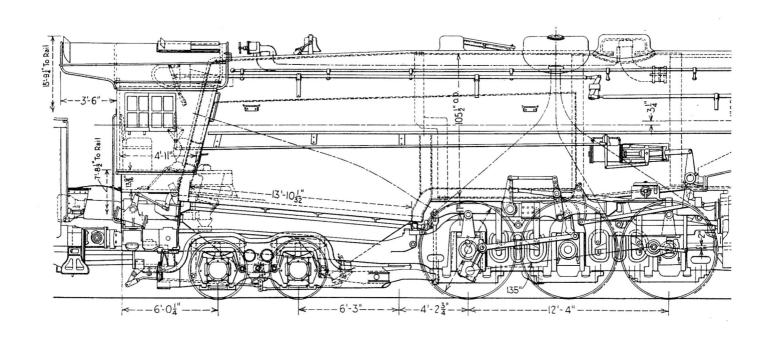

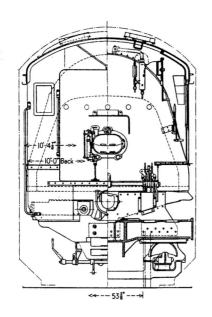
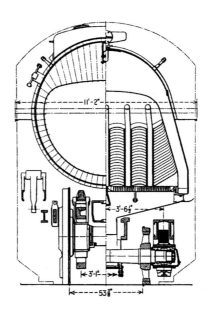
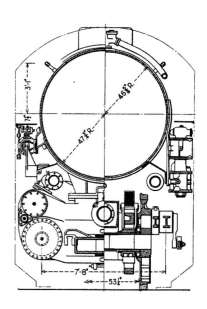

*Intended for fast freights, N&W had no compunction about using the 2-6-6-4s for other service as well when needed. Here an A with an auxiliary tender has some empty coal hoppers in tow at Suffolk, Virginia, about 1954. (H. Reid photo, TLC Collection)*

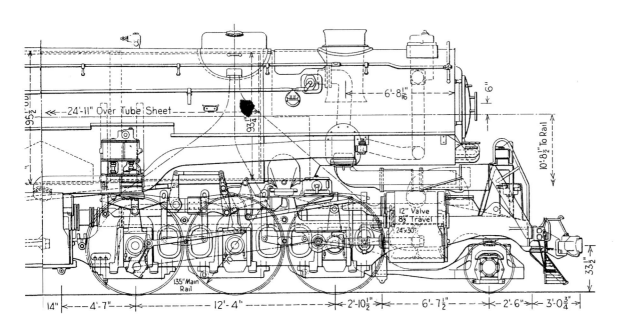

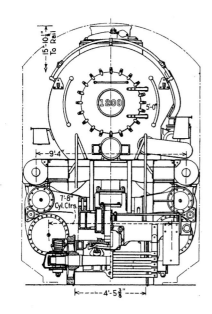

*No. 1207 sits shining in the sunlight on September 21, 1948, just outside the roundhouse in Norfolk. (TLC Collection)*

*Another location where the A-Class was often seen, and which was responsible for keeping them well-conditioned, was at Crewe, Virginia, midway on the run between Roanoke and Norfolk. Here No. 1207 sits at the Crewe yard at the very end of steam in 1959. (L. D. Lewis Collection)*

*This great overhead view at Blue Ridge on August 15, 1954, has No. 1238 with a time freight making a lot of exhaust as it challenges the grade. The auxiliary tender was regular for these locomotives, staring in the early 1950s. (Jay Williams collection)*

No. 1239, one of the newest A's, built in 1949, is handling an eastbound manifest freight at speed roaring past the Blue Ridge, Virginia station in March 1958. (H. H. Harwood Collection)

An empty coal train, normally the work of a Y Class, here is powered by A-Class No. 1214 and a J-Class 4-8-4 as the road engine. This is about as unusual a motive power alignment as one could imagine for the era: a passenger engine and a fast freight engine both working an empty coal train near Christiansburg, Virginia, in August 1956. (TLC Collection)

*No. 1221 takes empty hoppers back toward the coalfields with a cut of Clinchfield cars up front, westbound west of Bedford, Virginia, and ready to cross the Blue Ridge grade, in March 1958. ( H. H. Harwood photo)*

*Again in coal field service, No. 1221 is west of Bluefield with its auxiliary tender and string of empty hoppers in March 1958. (H. H. Harwood photo)*

No. 1240, one of the last A's and built in 1950, here leaves Roanoke with a manifest freight about 1954, while a passenger train sits by the platform in the background. (Jay Williams Collection)

The clean and face of No. 1240 is accentuated in its powerful appearance by the solid pilot, seen here at Shaffer's Crossing engine terminal at Roanoke in July 1956. (Joe Schmitz Photo, TLC Collection)

With empty hoppers, No. 1243, the very last A-class built, is hurrying west toward Blue Ridge in 1954. (John Krause Photo, TLC Collection)

The glint of the sun on the side of A-Class No. 1218 makes for a moody and artistic scene as it rolls westward at Kenova, West Virginia, in February 1956. ( H. H. Harwood photo)

Equipped for passenger train service, A-Class No. 1200 is seen here with Train No. 41, The New York, Chattanooga & New Orleans Limited, at Bristol, Virginia, having powered this Southern Railway train from Monroe over the N&W portion of its run. This July 1937 scene is just a year after the 1200 was built as the first of the class. The later A's saw considerable passenger service during World War II, both on troop specials and regular trains. No. 1200 has the as-built boiler tube pilot. (TLC Collection)

Making white exhaust as it gets underway, No. 104 is headed east from Columbus in September 1956. (Don Etter photo, Jay Williams Collection)

An N&W A-Class powers a coal train westward toward Portsmouth on the mainline, along the north bank of the Ohio River at Sciotoville, Ohio in September 1958. The C&O's giant Limeville (or Sciotoville) bridge carries its westbound main overhead. Both lines were used to transport coal to Columbus, and from there, to the Lakes or Midwestern connections. (John Krause Photo, TLC Collection)

No. 1208 is southbound out of Columbus as the engineer looks back at the photographer. (J. Parker Lamb photo)

No. 1204, with its original boiler-tube pilot, is wheeling a fast freight out of Columbus in the late 1930 or early 1940s. (TLC Collection)

A-Class No. 1029 pauses for servicing between runs under the rather small coaling station at Columbus in April 1958. (H. K. Vollrath Collection)

No. 1210 is setting off cars for the B&O at Chillicothe, Ohio on July 22, 1956. (TLC Collection)

No. 1218 boils out of the rainy mist of Tidewater Virginia with a train of empty hoppers for the coal fields in 1957. . . No wait it's 1987! Preserved No. 1218 is being ferried from Norfolk to Roanoke for excursion work later in the week. After a glorious and famous career hauling passenger excursions in the 1980s, No. 1218 today sleeps peacefully at the Virginia Transportation Museum in Roanoke. ( H. Reid photo, TLC Collection)

# 5: J Class – 4-8-4s

## The Famous Class J

Of all N&W steam motive power, the glamorous passenger hauling streamlined 4-8-4 perhaps has received the most attention and media coverage over the years, starting really at its birth in 1941.

N&W built 14 of these locomotives: Nos. 600-604 in 1941-42; Nos. 605-610 in 1943; and Nos. 611-613 in 1950. They fit the mode of the streamlined steam locomotive that became so popular with major railroads in the 1930s. The N&W's outlasted them all, finally ending their careers in 1958. N&W gave them class "J" in its steam roster scheme.

The 4-8-4 wheel arrangement was pioneered by Northern Pacific in 1927, when it purchased a number of these engines to handle its best passenger trains over steep grades. The type received quite a bit of press and was adopted and adapted by numerous railroads, so by the mid-1930s some railroad trade writers said it could possibly become the new "American Type." This harkened back to the 4-4-0 type that was so pervasive in early American railroading that it was called the American Type. Like the 4-4-0, the 4-8-4 had tremendous adaptability, with the flexibility, power, and speed to handle both fast freight and the best of passenger business. When the occasion warranted, the 4-8-4 could even do drag freight work. But, like the first Americans, it was best when fitted with high drivers and put to work on fast passenger trains.

The 4-8-4 was a natural outgrowth of the 4-8-2, and in total about 1,000 were built in the United States. N&W accounted for a tiny 1.4% of all 4-8-4s, yet in railroad literature, the N&W engines loom very large. The railroad trade press gave the name "Northern" to the 4-8-4 wheel arrangement because of its origins on the NP; many railroads had their own names for the type, probably more diverse names than any other wheel arrangement. N&W did not use names for its locomotive types, so on N&W they were simply the "J-Class."

The first J's had 275 psi boiler pressure, and with their 70-inch drivers, were rated at 73,300 pounds tractive effort. The last three of the class, built in 1950, had 300 psi and exerted 80,000 pounds of tractive effort, the most of any non-booster-equipped, single-expansion passenger locomotive.

Until 1941, N&W relied on the 4-8-2 Mountain-type for its heavy passenger work, supplemented by the 4-6-2 Pacific-type for secondary and branch lines. A few 4-4-2s and 4-6-0s from the early 1900s were also present into the 1930s, though the 4-4-2s were gone by 1934. A few of the 4-6-0s remained in service until after World War II. The 4-8-2s were first used on the N&W in 1916, and were its primary passenger power. However, a group of 10 of these locomotives were used primarily for freight (see Chapter 9).

By the late 1930s, after the steep dip in passenger travel during the early Depression years, there was a decided rebound and, overall, a great revival of interest in passenger trains by the major railroads across the country, in part because of the advent of the streamliner era. During the mid-to-late 1930s, a number of roads built new, lightweight stream-styled passenger trains and powered them with sleek, new diesels or streamlined steam.

A streamlined steam locomotive could be either a rebuild from an older engine or an all new engine. In either case the locomotive was encased in a cowl of some sort that gave it a streamlined appearance. Industrial engineers of high repute were hired to design these locomotives, including Henry Dreyfuss and Raymond Loewy on the NYC, PRR and other lines. Other railroads simply used their own imaginations. The results were sometimes pleasing and sometimes ugly.

N&W obviously wanted to improve it sagging fleet of passenger power by the late 1930s, and it had two nearby examples to study. The Richmond, Fredericksburg & Potomac Railroad, with a straight line, 113-mile railroad between Richmond and Washington, operated a large fleet of very heavy

*Official N&W diagram for the first J-Class engines (N&W Ry. Dated Aug. 23, 1941, TLC Collection)*

passenger trains. This line carried the Seaboard Air Line and Atlantic Coast Line railroads' Florida trains. It also handled their fast freights. In 1937, the RF&P acquired its first 4-8-4s and began building another series of engines in 1938 (finishing the class in 1945).

Since RF&P handled its freight at passenger speeds, the 4-8-4s were dual service. Nearby, in the Pocahontas Region, the C&O decided on the 4-8-4 type in 1935 and took possession of its first five locomotives for use between Charlottesville, Virginia, and Hinton, West Virginia. That route featured the heaviest grades on the mainline. There was plenty of operational data for N&W to study, both for fast-running (RF&P) and mountain operations (C&O).

N&W finally entered the 4-8-4 field in 1941, when the J class was built. By late 1941 it was evident that passenger traffic was surging. There was also a large increase in defense-type traffic to military bases being established in areas of Virginia served by N&W. These factors resulted in a decision to build streamlined 4-8-4s. Along with the new locomotive also came N&W's first streamlined passenger cars. The line did not buy entire new streamline train sets as the big passenger carriers did, but just a few streamlined cars to go along with the new J-Class.

The actual design of the locomotive was not from a highly-paid industrial designer, but by Frank C. Noel of the N&W's passenger car department. He designed a bullet-shaped nose, solid pilot, skyline casing, and running board skirting that satisfied management perfectly. The basic design was black, with a Tuscan Red stripe (to match the cars). Gold lettering covered the running board skirt and extended back along the tender to connect with the train. The design was not a "cowl," or "shroud," as with many streamlined steam designs. Instead, it followed the basic contours of the locomotive as it existed, so that it did not seem to be a box running down the line, but was simply a sleeker appearing object that was still instantly identifiable as a steam locomotive: cab, driving wheels, boiler, etc. The tenders were welded, so they had smooth sides, as opposed to the rivets seen on regular tenders.

The first Js were delivered in October 1941, just before the opening of America's war experience, and No. 604 was com-

*The cover and an inside advertisement from a typical N&W public timetable of the 1950s era featured the J prominently. (N&W Public Timetable Sept. 30, 1951)*

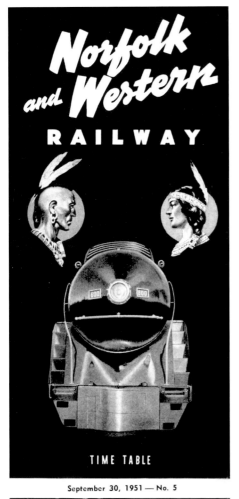

pleted in January 1942. They were ready for their great test during the war, when every bit of railroad equipment was utilized to the maximum. The last of the first five J's (No. 604) was given a booster that upped its starting tractive effort from 73,500 to 85,000 pounds. Why boosters were not applied to later locomotives is an open question. Apparently it was determined that they were not needed.

The 70-inch drivers were counterbalanced for speeds up to 140 mph. Among improvements were Nathan engine oil lubricators that forced lubrication to 208 points on the locomotive, and a value oil lubricator that provided lubrication to steam valves, pistons, etc. Pressure grease fittings added additional automatic lubrication.

The first five Js went to work on the *Pocahontas* (Trains 3 and 4) and the *Cavalier* (Trains 15 and 16), the two main name trains running Norfolk-Cincinnati. They usually covered these trains Norfolk-Roanoke-Williamson. They were also used on the Southern Railway trains that operated over the N&W between Monroe and Bristol.

To extend the runs of these locomotives to cover more trains over longer distances, N&W built an additional six in 1943. However, due to war-time restrictions they were classed as freight power and did not receive the streamlining feature. They were designated class J1. Numbered 605-610, they also had heavier reciprocating parts, again because of war-time restrictions. With these locomotives, the Js could cover the entire mainline name train fleet with a little to spare for the frequent additional sections and troop trains.

At the end of the war the J1 class was rebuilt with streamlining, new lightweight rods, etc. and re-classed as Js. They were now nearly identical to the first five.

A 1946 article in *Railway Mechanical Engineer* explains that the Js were used on Nos. 3, 4, 15, & 16 between Norfolk and Cincinnati, Nos. 17, 18, 45, 46, 41, & 42 (the latter four being Southern Railway through trains) between Monroe and Bristol. The article says:

"Shaffers Crossing engine terminal [Roanoke] is the home terminal for these locomotives, and the round trips of 504.6 miles

*Opposite: These four photos show locomotives of all three groups of the J-Class as they appeared in service and easily demonstrates their uniformity of appearance: No. 602 is at Cincinnati in October 1950; No. 606 is at Roanoke in January, 1944, illustrating its appearance as built as a non-streamlined J1 and then at Roanoke in August 1955 as a streamlined J; and No. 612 is at Bristol in June 1956 (J1, N&W photo, others Joe Schmitz photos, TLC Collection)*

The most complete history and best reference for the these locomotives is *Norfolk & Western Class J* by Kenneth L. Miller, Roanoke Chapter, NRHS, 2000, Roanoke, Virginia.

from that point to Norfolk, and 846.6 miles to Cincinnati and are typical of the runs. . . . With large capacity tenders and complete lubrication, service stops, except for those coincident with station stops, have almost been eliminated. An accompanying chart shows the assignment of the entire group of eleven locomotives at present time:"

| No. of Locos. | Train No. | Territory | Mileage |
|---|---|---|---|
| 2 | 4-15 and 16-3 | Roanoke-Norfolk | 1,008 |
| | 3-16 and 15-4 | Roanoke-Cincinnati | 1,696 |
| | | | |
| 8 | 17-46, 45-18 and 41-42 | Roanoke-Bristol | 906 |
| | 18-45 and 46-17 2/3 -- 2/4 | Roanoke-Williamson | 402 |
| | | | |
| Total Daily Mileage -- 10 locomotives | | | 4,244 |
| Average per locomotive | | | 424 |
| | | | |
| 1 | 42--41 | Roanoke-Monroe | 116 |
| | 2/4--2/3 | Roanoke-Crewe | 248 |
| Total Daily Mileage--11 locomotives | | | 4,608 |
| Average per locomotive | | | 419 |

This pattern changed when extra war-time runs between Crewe and Williamson were discontinued. The J class had done its duty well during the war emergency and was set to continue as N&W met postwar needs of its region.

In 1946, N&W introduced the first post-war streamliner, the *Powhatan Arrow*. It was the rail line's new all-coach fast flagship train between Norfolk and Cincinnati, and, of course, the Js were in charge. First using rebuilt cars, the train made a grand show and got the line much publicity.

With all new luxury cars being introduced on the *Arrow*, three additional J-Class 4-8-4s were built at Roanoke in 1950 to handle the extra business. The *Powhatan Arrow* received more advertising and got a great deal of publicity from the public and the railroad trade press; the image of the streamlined J was forever implanted in the public mind as the image of the N&W.

The last three Js were like their earlier sisters, except the boiler pressure was raised to 300 psi and the tractive effort went to 80,000 pounds, the highest of any non-booster-equipped passenger engine in the country. Soon, the other 11 J's had their boiler pressure increased as well. They continued handling the line's passenger trains, appearing on its timetables and in many of its ads, and generally were the stars of the late steam era.

There might have been some thinking when dieselization

began that the Js could stay in operation on passenger trains for some time to come, given their efficiency of operations. However, when the final decision to completely dieselize was made in 1958, they were precipitously kicked off the passenger trains and replaced by leased RF&P and ACL E7 and E8 diesels until N&W's own passenger diesels arrived. These were passenger-equipped GP9 EMD diesels, an ugly and odd-looking locomotive for a passenger train. But it was the way of the world then.

Some of the Js ran out their last year or so in local freight service. What a fall from grace! They were all retired for scrap between October 1958 and August 1959, with the exception of No. 611, which N&W saved and donated to the city of Roanoke. It later was transferred to the Virginia Transportation Museum. In 1981 it was refurbished and until 1995 operated numerous excursion trips on the new NS system, until retired again to the museum where it sits on display at this writing (2013). Its later-day excursion work only brought new luster to the sterling career of the class.

*A rarely seen overhead view shows inside the skyline casing of a typical J. This one was photographed at Williamson, West Virginia in the summer of 1956 (Gene Huddleston photo, Ron's Rosenberg Collection)*

## Specifications - J Class (1941)

### Weights:

| | |
|---|---|
| Lead Truck: | 90,000 lbs. |
| Drivers: | 288,000 lbs. |
| Trailer: | 116,000 lbs |
| Total Engine | 494,000 lbs. |
| Tender: | 378,600 lbs |

### Wheels:

| | |
|---|---|
| Leading Truck: | 36 inches |
| Drivers: | 70 inches |
| Trailer: | 42 inches |

| | |
|---|---|
| Cylinders: | 27x32 inches |
| Boiler Pressure: | 275 pounds per square inch |

### Heating Surface:

| | |
|---|---|
| Tubes & Flues: | 4,693 sq. ft. |
| Firebox, Comb. Chamber & Arch Tubes. | 578 sq. ft. |
| Superheater: | 2,177 sq. ft. |
| Total | 7,448 sq. ft. |
| Grate Area: | 107.7 sq. ft. |
| Firebox Inside: | 8 ft. -1 in x 12 ft. 2 in. |

| | |
|---|---|
| Superheater: | Type E |
| Stoker: | Standard Type HT |
| Valve Gear: | Baker |
| Throttle: | American Multiple |
| Feedwater Heater: | Worthington Type 65-A |
| Tractive Effort: | 73,300 lbs. |

No. 601 is ready to leave Norfolk's Terminal Station in 1955 with Train No. 3, the westbound *Pocahontas. It is about to make its run to Roanoke (252.3 miles), where it will be handed over to another J-Class for the remainder of the trip to Cincinnati (424.3 miles). (Don Wood photo, Ron Rosenberg Collection)*

J No. 602 with No. 3, the *Pocahontas, is making fast time on the straight line between Norfolk and Petersburg just out of Norfolk's Terminal Station in 1952, with 10 cars in tow and a great exhaust of white steam. (Jay Williams Collection)*

N&W handled four Southern Railway through trains between its connection with the SR near Lynchburg, Virginia, and Bristol, Virginia/Tennessee. The Js were stationed at SR's large Monroe yard just north of Lynchburg, where they picked up the SR trains. Here SR Train No. 45, the *Tennessean, is being powered by J-Class No. 610 as it leaves Monroe on June 9, 1946. The 610 is one of the Js built in 1943 without streamlining. This was added by the time this photo was made. (TLC Collection)*

With N&W's iconic Hotel Roanoke in the background, No. 611, today (2013) the last survivor of the class, heads eastbound with No. 4 in the early 1950s. (Jay Williams Collection)

A J class leaving Bristol with the northbound Tennessean (No. 46). The train is headed for Monroe, where it will be taken over by SR diesels for the remainder of its trip to Washington. The nine cars of mixed heritage in the train will be no problem for the big J as it crosses the Blue Ridge en route. (TLC Collection)

*Local No. 24 called at Elliston, Virginia, at 2:10 p.m. with its RPO, two full express cars, combine, and coach as it made its all-stops local run from Williamson to Roanoke with No. 606 in charge. The date is May 10, 1954. The J was at home on local runs such as this, as well as pulling the big name trains, though this was a gross underutilization of its power. (Jay Williams Collection)*

*No. 607 is wheeling the westbound* Powhatan Arrow *(No. 26) just outside of Christiansburg, Virginia, in June 1958 during the last days of the Js in passenger service. (H. H. Harwood photo)*

*This famous N&W publicity photo shows the new* Powhatan Arrow *running along the New River near Parrott, Virginia, west of Roanoke, with No. 607 leading. Used in many advertisements, this is one of the iconic J-Class action official photos. (N&W Ry. Photo, TLC Collection)*

*New Year's Day, 1958 finds a J-Class with a heavy train leaving Bluefield in a show of wintry exhaust. (William Gordon photo)*

*On the cold night of March 28, 1958, No. 606 with a night train exits Montgomery Tunnel. (William Gordon photo)*

*No. 605 pauses with the Cavalier at Williamson, West Virginia, in April 1957. By this date, the Cavalier's main duty was to move the mail and express over the road. The train had a lot more of that cargo than passengers, as this photo attests. (Jim Shaw photo, TLC Collection)*

*This is No. 4, the* Pocahontas, *at Roanoke on July 18, 1958. Nothing unusual about the scene except it was the very last regular run of steam on an eastbound N&W train. (N&W Ry. Photo, TLC Collection)*

*No. 26, the eastbound* Powhatan Arrow *is eastbound with No. 605 and six cars under the wires of N&W electrified territory ay May-beury, West Virginia, on June 19, 1949. (Richard J. Cook photo, TLC Collection)*

*No. 603 cuts the ribbon on the new Elkhorn Tunnel on its opening date June 26, 1950, with the eastbound Powhatan Arrow. Such an important occasion demanded a polished J with the flagship Arrow, rather than some work-a-day Y or even an A. (N&W Ry. Photo, TLC Collection)*

*No. 606 has the* Arrow *leaving Ironton, Ohio, eastbound in 1953. (Gene Huddleston photo, TLC Collection)*

No. 605 takes the all-coach and no-checked-baggage Powhatan Arrow out of Cincinnati Union Terminal in October 1954. The skirts on the cars will soon be removed for convenience in maintenance. (J. J. Young photo, TLC Collection)

The 606 hurries along westbound toward Cincinnati near Coal Grove, Ohio, in August 1957. One can just feel the speed in this photo. Look at the clear stack! (Jay William Collection)

No. 600 is seen here in its last days as a local freight engine at Gray, Virginia, in late 1958. Soon even this task was dieselized and the 600, first of its breed, would retire. (H. Reid photo, TLC Collection)

# 6: G and W Classes – 2-8-0s

The Consolidation type (2-8-0) locomotive was the most commonly used wheel arrangement in American railroading, aggregating a total of over 33,000 engines built. N&W bought Consolidations first in 1883 and used them consistently for general freight service until they were eclipsed by a number of new arrivals starting with the first of the 4-8-0s in 1906, and then the Mallets in the following decades. N&W would eventually have about 450 2-8-0s, but most of them were gone by time period of this book.

| Class | Built | on Roster: | | |
|-------|-------|------|------|------|
|       |       | 1930 | 1944 | 1951 |
| G-1   | 6     | 6    | 6    | 2    |
| W-1   | 65    | 3    | 0    | 0    |
| W-2   | 196   | 97   | 44   | 9    |

The 2-8-0 types gained acceptance in American railroading as a natural follow-on for the 4-6-0 ten wheeler, which was used in dual passenger and freight service up to the early 1880s on most railroads. The additional driver, and a long narrow firebox with generally small diameter drivers identified these are strictly freight-hauling locomotives. N&W started with the long firebox, but eventually enlarged it and placed it over the last set of drivers, thus improving on the earlier 2-8-0 designs.

The 2-8-0s were first purchased with N&W's opening of the Pocahontas coal fields in West Virginia with the need for heavier power to carry this developing traffic eastward. Purchases continued through the next two decades, and included such anomalies as Baldwin Vauclain compound types and Richmond cross-compound types, all in an effort to develop more power more efficiently in individual locomotives. Some were bought strictly for pusher service on the grade through Elkhorn Tunnel, others were used in fast freight service, and were quite adequate for the traffic of the era, especially on the lower grade areas of the road.

By the turn of the 20th Century most railroads were beginning to develop motive power that suited their particular needs rather than to buy the standard designs that were being built in the 1890s, both in passenger and freight engines. N&W got 4-4-2s, 4-6-0s, and later 4-8-2s for passenger work, and for freight started with the 2-8-0 and then opted in a big way for the compound articulated Mallet types starting with the 2-6-6-2s and then developing the ever-better Y-class series of 2-8-8-2s, as well as the 4-8-0s.

The 2-8-0s found themselves bumped from the mainline freight runs with the coming of these new types, and eventually they were relegated to branch line, local, and yard work. Many were scrapped as the newer types arrived, and by the late 1930s only a remnant of the once large fleet remained. These continued to be retired piecemeal as newer locomotives arrived in more and more quantity until those that were left had been relegated almost exclusively to yard work as switch engines. This policy was not different than that followed by many other railroads as they downgraded older locomotives for use in yards and for industrial switching. In these duties several of the 2-8-0s survived until after World War II, but in 1950 N&W bought 30 almost brand new ex-C&O 0-8-0 purpose-built switchers and then built no less than 45 almost exact copies at the Roanoke Shops. These efficient new locomotives took over all switching work, and the few remaining 2-8-0s were retired, until there were four in service in 1956. Some of the W-1 2-8-0s were converted to saddle-tank engines for use as shop switchers, lasting to 1956 or later.

During the era of our treatment in the last 30 years of N&W steam operations, the surviving 2-8-0s were almost exclusively used in switching, with some used on light branches. Nos. 6 and 7 lasted until 1954 on the Abingdon Branch – they were G-1's built in 1897. The 2-8-0 numbers declined steadily in the 1930-50s era, so that by 1945 only 21 remained on the active

*N&W mechanical diagram showing the G-1 class 2-8-0s. The G-1s were built in 1880s and 1890s. Nos. 6 & 7 lasted until 1954 on the Abingdon Branch. (TLC Collection)*

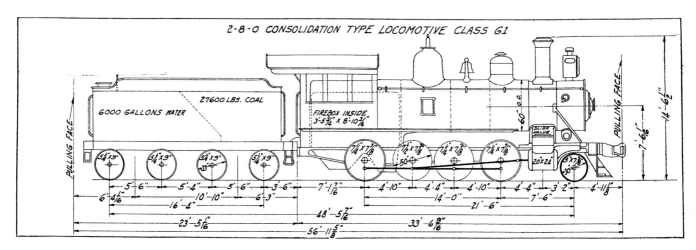

The 2-8-0s came in several classes, subclasses and revised classes. They were rebuilt, dimensions changed, appliances added, and adjustments made such that any study of this would require an almost-book length treatment. Suffice it to say for this book that the 2-8-0s in last 30 years of steam were present in yards and on some branch lines, but were hardly noticeable in the overall N&W motive power picture.

*No. 306 was a G-1 class built by Baldwin in 1889. It was finally retired in 1934, and is seen here at Roanoke a few years before, on July 10, 1931. The tall capped stack was an anachronism by the time of this photo and reminded one of 19th Century design. (TLC Collection)*

*A second photo shows No. 306 working in the Raonoke yards in 1930. The photo gives a good profile of this ancient-looking machine. (TLC Collection)*

*N&W mechanical diagram showing the W-2 class 2-8-0s. The W-2s were the largest class of 2-8-0s and several survived into the later era in switching work. (TLC Collection)*

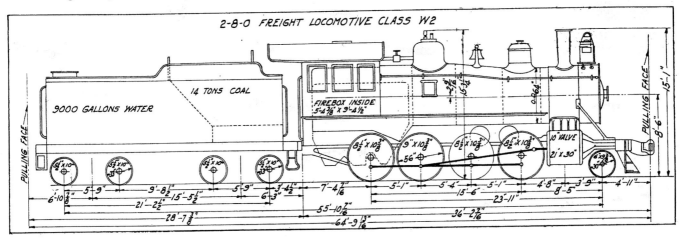

W-2 No. 686 is at the Kenova, West Virginia, terminal on July 11, 1934. The engine lasted only a year after this photo was taken, as it was retired in November 1935. (TLC Collection)

W-2 No 695, built by Alco's Richmond Works in 1905, is seen here at Roanoke on August 31, 1930. It lasted until May 1950 and was one of the last 2-8-0s on the N&W, finally bumped from its switching duties by the new 0-8-0s. (TLC Collection)

W-2 No 674 is another of the class that worked until the new 0-8-0s arrived, seen here stored at Norfolk just before its retirement in April 1950. (TLC Collection)

No. 690, another long-lived W-2, was built by Richmond in 1905 and served until the 0-8-0s arrived. It was retired to scrap soon after this April 15, 1950 photo showed it still active at the Lynchburg yard. (A. A. Thieme Photo, TLC Collection)

No. 885 is seen here in switching work at Petersburg on September 25, 1947. It was a strong locomotive that was adept at fairly heavy switching work. N&W made good use of its older engines in this way, not opting for a large batch of purpose-built switchers until the last decade of steam. No. 885 was retied in October 1949. (L. M. Kelley photo, TLC Collection)

W-2 No. 735 switches at Lambert's Point in Norfolk May 6, 1936, its pilot having been adapted with the footboards long before, but otherwise looking much the same as it had in road freight service. It was in service until the coming of the 0-8-0s and went to scrap in April 1950. (Bruce D. Fales photo, TLC Collection)

No. 701 was another graduate of Richmond in 1905 that worked until the end, seen here at Lambert's Point September 3, 1949. It was scrapped the following year with arrival of the 0-8-0s. (A. A. Thieme photo, TLC Collection)

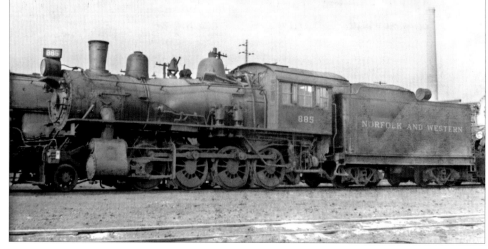

No. 885 was a Richmond product from 1902 that was not retired until October 1949. It is seen here at Roanoke in September 1949 going about it accustomed yard work. (George Votava photo, TLC Collection)

*Working in the Bristol yard on January 27, 1935, No. 771 has the characteristic footboards on the pilot and the backup headlight on the tender. It persisted in this work until 1945. (TLC Collection)*

*A Cooke Works product of 1903, W-2 No. 940 is at work at Petersburg Sept. 25, 1947, a year before its retirement. (L. M. Kelley photo, TLC Collection)*

# 7: M Classes – 4-8-0s

N&W had the largest fleet of 4-8-0 types in America, with 286, all built between 1906 and 1912. They were an all-purpose freight locomotive for N&W, and many, especially the later-built ones, continued working into the last decade of steam in the 1950s. Those constructed in 1906-07 received road numbers 375-499 and were classified "M." Those built later in 1907 (1000-1099) got M-1 Class, and the last batch, numbers 1100-1160, built in 1910-12, were given M-2 Class.

The 4-8-0 wheel arrangement is fairly rare on American Railroads, with about 600 built in the United States. That means that almost half of them were owned by N&W. The type was first called "Mastodon," but on N&W they were simply Twelve-Wheelers. Some employees called them "Bullmoose," for whatever reason. Of course, they were new on the road when Teddy Roosevelt was making his Bullmoose third-party run for the presidency.

The first 4-8-0 appeared on the Lehigh Valley Railroad about 1870. It was built as an experiment to raise the boiler capacity and riding stability of the 2-8-0. The type had some acceptance on the Central Pacific (later Southern Pacific) for mountain work in the 1880s-90s, and it was constructed by commercial builders up to about 1910.

N&W bought its first 4-8-0s from Alco's Richmond Works, a comparable batch from Baldwin, and then smaller groups from both Richmond and Baldwin before building the last 11 at Roanoke Shops in 1912.

By the turn of the 20th century N&W was handling its heaviest freights with 2-8-0s, and passenger trains with 4-4-0s and 4-6-0s. It was in the first decade of that century that the road began to plan and develop power specific to its needs. For freight the N&W adopted the 4-8-0 beginning in 1906, and completed its fleet in 1912. At the end of this period it began to buy into the Mallet compound articulated design heavily and that would be its track going forward.

N&W was just a few years ahead of the arrival on the motive power scene of the 2-8-2 Mikado-type locomotive. The Mikado was also an outgrowth of the 2-8-0, adding a trailing truck to support a much enlarged fire box. It began to be built about 1906, at the very same time that N&W started with the 4-8-0 type. The Mikado (named because the first production run of engines went to the Japanese National Railways) became a standard general purpose freight locomotive on most other railroads, many of which had large numbers. About 13,000 2-8-2s were built in America, and they were undoubtedly the most popular freight type in the 1910-1930 era.

However, N&W was committed to its 4-8-0 concept and stayed with it until the Mallets began to meet the needs of heavier work. N&W stands as one of the very few major railways that did not have at least some 2-8-2s.

Happy with the 4-8-0s, N&W put them to work on all types of freight. Once the 2-8-8-2s were in service in qualities, the 4-8-0s ended heavy coal train work, and were used on fast freights, locals, branches and, eventually, in yard service as hand-me-down switchers as they aged. In the 1920s they could handle a 5,400-ton coal train between Crewe and Nor-

*Official N&W Diagram Sheet for M-2 class dated June 27, 1938.*

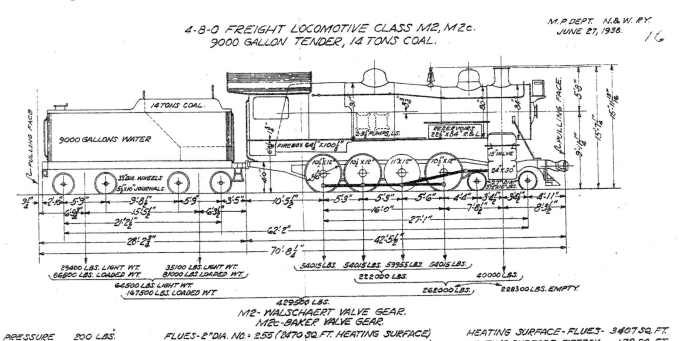

folk, and in manifest freight train service they could pull 4,500 tons eastbound (and about a third of that westbound) between these two points, which had no long, steep grades. They also had the manifest freight work on the line Portsmouth-Columbus-Cincinnati. They could drag 2,400 tons on trains between Portsmouth and Columbus.

The 4-8-0s were eclipsed in main freight work by new 4-8-2s, and, of course, by the soon-to-be ubiquitous 2-8-8-2s. Many were scrapped and those left were relegated to branch lines with light axle load requirements, local freights, and general switching duties. Their numbers diminished though the late 1920s and 1930s, with a smaller number retired in the 1940s. Several lasted to the very end of steam; almost an anachronism when seen beside the giant Y-6 or Super Power A-class.

The road numbers were:

| Class | Numbers | Built |
|---|---|---|
| M | 375-499 | 1906-1907 Richmond and Baldwin |
| M1 | 1000-1099 | 1907 Richmond and Baldwin |
| M2 | 1100-1149 | 1911 Baldwin |
| M2a | 1150-1160 | 1911-1912 Roanoke Shops |

(All but 1150-1160 were built commercially. The last 11 were Roanoke products.)

Two of the class were rebuilt in an experiment with an "Automatic" switcher in 1947. (See chapter 10)

Retirements were as follows:
M and M-1 Classes (375-1099):
Retired in the 1920s: 85 locomotives
Retired in the 1930s: 76 locomotives
Retired in the 1940s: 30 locomotives
Retired in the 1950s: 31 locomotives

The M1s were the first to be retired, because the N&W didn't like their Walschaerts valve gear.

All the M-2 Class (1100-1160) lasted until scrapping in 1951-1957 period (except 1140, which was sold to Durham & Southern Railroad in 1939).

Mechanically the M and M-1 classes were virtual duplicates except in a few areas, such as valve gear, etc. However, the M-2 class was larger and more powerful.

## Specifications:

This is a typical specification taken from an M-2 class with information dated June 27, 1938:

**Weights:**

| | |
|---|---|
| Lead Truck: | 40,000 lbs. |
| Drivers: | 222,000 lbs. |
| Total Engine | 262,000 lbs. |
| Tender: | 14-Tons, 9,000 gallons |

**Wheels:**

| | |
|---|---|
| Leading Truck: | 27 inches |
| Drivers: | 56 inches |
| Cylinders: | 24x30 inches |
| Boiler Pressure: | 200 pounds per square inch |

**Heating Surface:**

| | |
|---|---|
| Flues: | 3,407 sq. ft. |
| Firebox: | 179 sq. ft. |
| Superheater: | 765 sq. ft. |
| Total | 4,351 sq. ft. |
| Grate Area: | 45 sq. ft. |
| Firebox Inside: | 64-1/4 in. x 100-1/8 in. |
| Tractive Effort | 52,457 lbs. |

Class M No. 475 survives and is alive and well at the Strassburg RR in Pennsylvania, where it runs on occasion.

*Class M No. 376 was the second 4-8-0 built for N&W, in 1906, and is shown here at Norton, Virginia, on September 9, 1947. It was not retired until March 1958, at the very end of steam. It survived longer than any other Class M- 4-8-0 and can certainly be called the exemplar of the type.*

*Whether in mine shifter or yard work, this was a versatile locomotive. (L. M. Kelley photo, TLC Collection)*

*With its capped stack, No. 382 is wheeling the Abington Branch mixed train along that bucolic line in the summer of 1954. (John Krause Photo, TLC Collection)*

*No. 392 is switching at Columbus on October 10, 1947. It still has five years of life left. (Clyde E, Helms photo, TLC Collection).*

No. 396, another M Class from the first order, has a rebuilt tender with six-wheel trucks in this December 29, 1952 photo at Shaffer's Crossing terminal in Roanoke. Another long-lasting engine, it was retired in July 1958. (C. W. Witbeck photo, TLC Collection)

No. 422 also has a tender sporting six-wheel trucks in this switching action photo at Columbus in October 1953. (Jay Williams Collecting)

Another stout switcher, No. 433 is resting between duties at Shaffer's Crossing on July 26 1947. (TLC Collection)

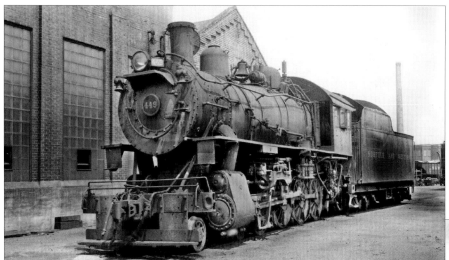

Stored at Radford, Virginia, in July 1957, No. 449 will be retired for scrap in December of that year. (R. D. Patton Photo)

The hostler is busying around No. 457 at Kenova, West Virginia, where the sturdy 4-8-0 is being used for heavy switching duties. N&W had a major loading point for Ohio River barges here. The date is October 9, 1949. (C. T. Felstead photo)

This high-angle view gives an appreciation of how the M Class looked from the top. It is at Christiansburg on September 2, 1957, ready to take a railfan excursion of 13 cars up the branch to Blacksburg as part of a triple header. That must have been a great NRHS Convention that year. (TLC Collection)

*M-Class No. 488 is at the Radford yard on December 30, 1952. This particular angle gives a good appreciation for the classic early-20th century lines of the engine with its roomy cab, tapered boiler, high domes and stack. (C. W. Witbeck Photo)*

*No. 496 works the Columbus yard in this July 1957 picture. This long-lasting engine had another year of work ahead of it. (Joe Schmitz Photo)*

*No. 1090, an M-1 class, built by Alco-Richmond in in 1907, is seen here in yard work at Columbus July 23, 1933. It was retired only two years after this photo, in 1935. (TLC Collection)*

The scene is at Clare yard, N&W's Cincinnati terminal, as M-2 Class No. 1107 rests between switching duties on September 25, 1938. (Robert J. Foster Photo)

No. 119 still has its standard boiler-tube pilot and a larger tender in this photo from May 28, 1935 at Hagerstown. (Bruce Fales photo, TLC Collection)

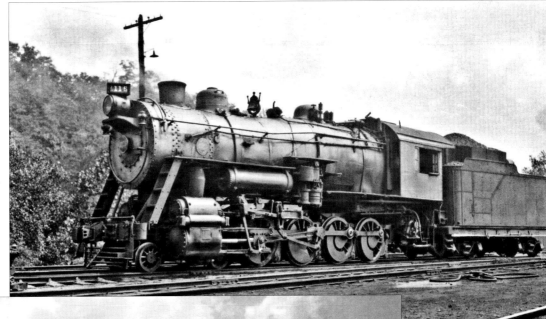

*These two photos show M-2 No. 1115. The first is at Lynchburg, Virginia, March 30, 1930 and second is at Hagerstown, Maryland, August 19, 1941. Note that in that year the engine has been given a larger, N&W-standard tender. It may have been that in the latter scene the No. 1115 was in local freight work on the Shenandoah Valley line. (both, TLC Collecting)*

*The tender of No. 1128 has a built-up coal bunker, and the engine is remarkably clean in this August 14, 1949 photo at Lynchburg. (A. A. Thieme photo, TLC Collection)*

*No. 1148 has the larger six-wheel tender in this scene at Shenandoah, Virginia, on August 16, 1953. It was sold to Wise Coal & Coke Company in February 1957. (TLC Collection)*

*M-2 No. 1153 has an enlarged tender with six-wheel trucks in this photo at Clare yard in Cincinnati on August 24, 1947. (Robert Graham Photo, TLC Collection)*

*No. 1143 is on a local freight at Chillicothe, Ohio, on August 16, 1938. These versatile locomotives were adept at jobs such as this. (C. E. Helms Photo, TLC Collection)*

## 8: E Class – 4-6-2s

N&W rostered a total of 63 4-6-2 Pacific-type locomotives in Classes E-1, E-2 (and E-2a and E-2b), and E-3. The first came in 1905, followed by the rest in 1907, 1910, 1912, 1913, and 1914. All 20 E-1 Class 4-6-2s were retired in the 1930s, and by the end of 1950, there were just 12 Pacific types left on N&W. No. 563 was the very last of the type retired, in December 1958.

The 4-6-2 was a direct outgrowth of the old 4-6-0 Ten Wheeler that was a dual freight/passenger design very widely used on American railroads in the last two decades of the 19th century. It was built from 1902 through about 1930 and for that period, was more or less the standard passenger power on most railroads; over 6,300 were built for use in the United States.

Some lines used the Pacific as a fast freight locomotive for short manifest runs, but it was most generally a passenger type. The wheel arrangement was first used on the Missouri Pacific and Chesapeake & Ohio in 1902. C&O sought to call it a "Mountain Type," but the railroad trade press named it "Pacific Type," after the MoPac locomotives, and the name stuck.

N&W was quick to buy Pacifics, with its first E-1 class arriving in 1905. They supplanted 4-6-0s on the heaviest passenger trains in the territory with the steepest grades, in company with 4-4-2 Atlantic types (which N&W acquired in 1903-04). The 4-4-2s handled trains on the runs east of Crewe to Norfolk and in Ohio, while the 4-6-2s took over the mountain duties

west of Crewe. The first five E-Class 4-6-2s were built by Alco's Richmond Works in 1905. They were followed by 16 more from Baldwin in 1907. The E-1s had 68-inch drivers and exerted 28,000 pounds of tractive effort.

When the 16 E-2 class engines were delivered from Richmond in 1910, they were larger, with 34,425 pounds of tractive effort and 70-inch drivers. Six more of the E-2s arrived from Baldwin in 1912, and N&W's Roanoke Shops turned out 15 in 1912-14 (originally called E-2b, most were later re-entered into the E-2a class). These were the last of the type on the N&W, with the exception of the five locomotives in the E-3 class, which N&W purchased secondhand from the Pennsylvania Railroad in 1930. Most of the E-2 and E-2b Class were given superheaters and reclassified as E-2a.

This fine fleet of Pacifics became standard passenger power on the N&W, but there was an almost immediate recognition that a larger locomotive might be needed in the near future, because of the quick advent of the steel passenger car. American railroads begin to replace wooden and composite cars (cars with steel under-frames and posts with wooden bodies) with all-steel cars for safety reasons starting about 1905. The replacements proceeded very quickly and, as a result, the need for larger passenger engines was felt. For N&W, this resulted in adoption of the 4-8-2 Mountain Type, first developed in 1911 by neighboring C&O in conjunction with Alco's Richmond plant.

As Mountain types carried the heavier train over the heaviest grades, the Pacifics were relegated to secondary and branch

*Official N&W mechanical diagram sheet for the E-2a, E-b Pacific Type dated June 30, 1938, showing the engine with a 20-ton, 12,000 gallon tender. Others of the E-2 and E-2a Types had 16-ton, 12,000 gallon tenders. The E-1s had the original small 14-ton, 9,000 gallon tenders. (TLC Collection)*

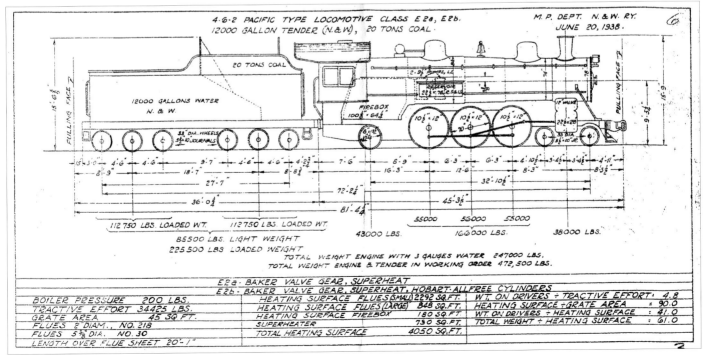

lines, and low-grade areas of the system. By the last decade the Pacifics worked out of Bluefield and in southwestern Virginia and West Virginia coal field branches, plus other local work. They were notably used on the Cannonball trains operating Norfolk-Richmond (via the ACL between Petersburg and Richmond). They were almost exclusive power on the Lynchburg-Durham trains.

The 4-4-2 Atlantics continued in use east of Crewe until about 1930, when N&W purchased five Pacific types secondhand from the Pennsylvania Railroad. These 4-6-2s were given E-3 class. With 80-inch drivers, they were most suitable for low-grade routes where speed was of more interest than power. They exerted 38,283 pounds of traction. From the time of their arrival they handled the heaviest trains on the Norfolk-Crewe run, and on trains N&W ran between Norfolk and Petersburg, and over the Atlantic Coast Line tracks to and from Richmond. They also held down runs in the west out of Portsmouth to Columbus and Cincinnati, but were replaced by 4-8-2s relatively quickly. They were all scrapped in 1946-47.

Roster:

| | | |
|---|---|---|
| 500-504 | Baldwin 1913 - From PPR to N&W 1930 | E-3 |
| 543-552 | Roanoke Shops - 1913-1914 | E-2a, E-2b |
| 553-558 | Baldwin - 1912 | E-2a |
| 559-563 | Roanoke Shops - 1912 | E-2a |
| 564-579 | Alco - Richmond - 1910 | E-2, E-2a |
| 580-594 | Baldwin - 1907 | E-1 |
| 595-599 | Alco - Richmond - 1905 | E-1 |

This photo shows 4-6-2 No. 552 at speed with the "Cannonball" train on the Atlantic Coast Line tracks near Richmond. The 4-6-2s often made this run in the later years, along with streamlined 4-8-2s. The train operated on N&W Norfolk-Petersburg and then ran as a joint N&W/ACL train (with cars from both lines) on ACL to Richmond's Broad Street Station. (J. I. Kelly photo)

By 1930, the threshold date for the book's coverage, all the 4-6-0 Ten Wheelers had been scrapped, but all seven 4-4-2s (built in 1903 and classed "J") were still in service. However, they were finally bumped from the runs they held by 4-6-2s in 1930, with the arrival of the five secondhand PRR engines. All seven of the Atlantics were scrapped between 1931 and 1935. When they were gone, the "J" Class became vacant, which was filled in 1941 by a much more famous N&W locomotive type.

As classic a turn-of-the-century passenger engine as one could find, the N&W's beautifully proportioned, high-stepping 4-4-2s were soon enough bested by the 4-6-2 types which arrived almost concurrently. Here No. 601 is at Norfolk July 3, 1932. It was retired in 1935. (TLC Collection)

This great, sharp photo shows a highly polished No. 546 at Norton, Virginia, on September 19, 1947. In their later years, the 4-6-2s often conducted the passenger runs in southwestern Virginia west of Bluefield. The 546 was one of only 15 of the N&W's 63 Pacific Types built by the Roanoke Shops, the balance having come from Alco and Baldwin. (L. M. Kelley photo)

Out of Welch, E-2a No. 554 is power for mixed train No. 157 as it rounds a horseshoe curve at Black Wolfe, on the Tug Fork Branch, headed for the West Virginia town of Jenkinjones, in 1947. (TLC Collection)

No. 556 heads up a short local at Lynchburg, Virginia, in 1948, probably the train from Durham. It was a Baldwin product, from the order delivered in 1912. (Jay Williams Collection)

No. 553 awaits its next assignment at Petersburg on September 23, 1947. It was one of five 4-6-2s built at Roanoke during N&W's quick acquisition of its fleet of Pacifics in the 1905-1913 period. It was the last 4-6-2 retired, in December 1958. (L. M. Kelley Photo)

No. 578 (built at Richmond in 1910) is seen here westbound out of Bluefield with a train headed down the line to Norton, about 1948. (Ray Tobey Photo)

A good overhead view of No. 578, with an auxiliary tender, is on a local train near Tazewell, Virginia, in June 1958. This particular locomotive was given to the Ohio Railroad Museum in Worthington (Columbus) and is there today. (J. Parker Lamb photo)

Two more views of No. 578 find it inside the Bluefield Lubratorium shop in May 1958, during its last days of active use. (J. Parker Lamb photos)

No. 582, an E-1 from Baldwin in 1907 is shown here with the Cannonball near Richmond on ACL tracks about 1948. (J. I. Kelly photo)

Down on the Lynchburg & Durham line, No. 556 has two-car train No. 36 in tow, leaving Durham Union Station in the 1930s. It departed there at 1:45 p.m. and arrived in Lynchburg at 5:15 p.m. By this time the 4-6-2s were handling locals, and no longer seeing service on the name trains. (TLC Collection)

Though lettered N&W, No. 500 had the unmistakable lines of a PRR Pacific. It is being readied for a run to Portsmouth on an N&W mainline passenger train in May 6, 1938. (Bruce Fales photo, TLC Collection)

Another assignment that the ex-PRR Pacifics handled was the Shenandoah Valley line. Here No. 504 is leaving Hagerstown with a five-car train. (TLC Collection)

# 9: K Class – 4-8-2s

The 4-8-2 wheel arrangement was a natural outgrowth of the 4-6-2. It simply added more weight, an extra set of driving wheels, and a longer, larger boiler. However, the two-wheel trailing truck did not allow for a sufficiently enlarged firebox and sometimes the boiler had problems producing enough steam for all types of service.

As the name implies, these locomotives, with their added adhesion and power, were first used for heavy trains in mountain territory. The type was conceived by Chesapeake & Ohio in 1911 for use on its mountain territory between Charlottesville, Virginia, and Hinton, West Virginia, crossing some of the same mountains crossed just a few miles to the south by N&W. The type was quickly adopted by American railroads and became popular during the 1911-1930 era. About 2,400 were built.

The engine was dual service; easily at home on fast freights as well as heavy passenger manifests, but generally was most often seen pulling the latter. It was the foundation of the future 4-8-4, which added a much larger firebox and essentially perfected the eight-coupled locomotive for passenger and some freight applications.

The same thing that drove C&O to improve its heavy passenger locomotive fleet was also the impetus for N&W's acquisition of the 4-8-2 starting in 1916. Not only did management want more power for the mountain grades, which were far more severe than C&O's, but trains in this era were becoming much heavier. The increase in weight was not just from more patronage, but also because the steel under-frame composite cars that started service about 1900 gave way to all-steel cars after about 1905.

The steel cars made passenger trains decidedly heavier, requiring more powerful locomotives. There was always the option to double-head trains in the mountain territory, but this added a lot more cost. The development of a more powerful single locomotive was the obvious answer, and this need was met by the N&W in 1916.

N&W's K-1 Class had road number numbers 100-115 and was entirely home-built at Roanoke between 1916 and 1917, just in time to handle the highest-ever passenger loads during World War I. K-2 Class was numbered 116-125 and was built by Alco's Brooks Works in 1919. These locomotives followed the USRA design, since they were built during the period when USRA was managing the country's railroads.

*This heavily retouched 1933 publicity photo is of Mountain type No. 124 leading a passenger train at the New River Palisades near Pembroke, Virginia, and was used in ads and timetables in the 1930s period. (N&W Ry. Photo, TLC Collection)*

The K-2a Class came in 1923 from Baldwin Locomotive Works. It was a close copy of the K-2, with certain modifications that made it a USRA copy. The K-3 was the final order of 4-8-2s, and was designed strictly for freight service. These 10 engines (200-209) were built by Roanoke Shops in 1926.

N&W's first 38 Mountains were characteristically passenger engines, though they saw a share of freight business, whereas the 10 K-3s were built just for freight service. All 38 in the K-1, K-2, and K-2a Classes held out until the end of steam, and retired 1957-59. The 10 freight-only K-3s were sold

to power-hungry Richmond, Fredericksburg & Potomac (Nos. 200-205), and Denver & Rio Grande Western (206-209) in 1944. This was during the height of World War II rail traffic. They were later resold by these two roads to the Wheeling & Lake Erie. These old workhorses ended their lives as Nickel Plate Road engines, after W&LE merged into that line.

The Roanoke-built K-1s had 70-inch drivers, weighed 347,000 pounds and developed 57,200 pounds tractive effort, with boiler pressure of 200 psi. The K-1s were increased to 220 psi boilers and had Worthington Feedwater heaters added

*These three official N&W diagram drawings show the K-1, K-2, 2a, and K-3 N&W Mountain types. (TLC Collection)*

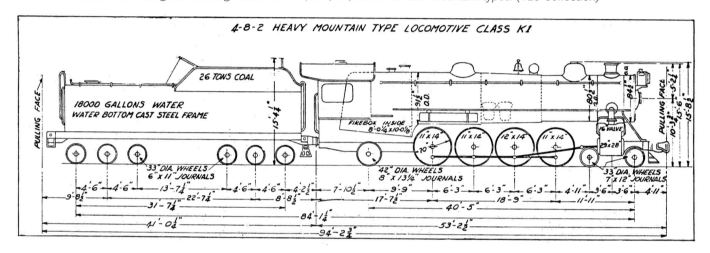

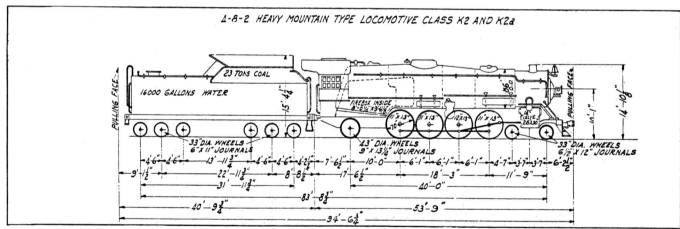

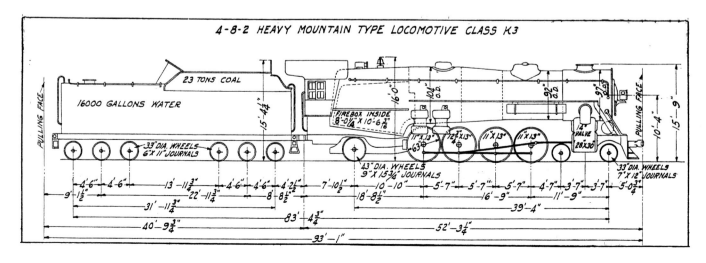

*K-1 No. 103 is power for the four-car Shenandoah Valley line local No. 13 at Buena Vista, Virginia, on June 5, 1935. The 4-8-2s were used on the Valley line throughout their lives. (Walter Thrall photo, TCL Collection)*

during rebuilding. They were then rated for 62,920 pounds starting tractive effort.

The K-2 Class was completed by Alco in 1919 and complied with the United States Railroad Administration (USRA) heavy 4-8-2 design, since the N&W, along with all other U. S. railroads, was still under federal control that began during World War I's heightened logistical needs. They had 69-inch drivers, weighed 352,000 pounds and exerted 58,000 pounds of tractive effort. As with the K-1, their boiler pressure was later raised to 220 psi and the tractive effort rating went to 63,800 pounds.

The K-3 Class was built by Roanoke Shops in 1923, and had an engine weight of 401,900 pounds. They had larger, 23-ton/16,000 gallon tenders. Their drivers were lower – 63 inches - because of their use as freight locomotives. They were intended strictly for use in fast freight service on the areas of the N&W system where the grades were not steep, and were designed to supplant the 4-8-0 type in this service. The 4-8-0s were proving too small for the work, requiring double-heading at times. The belief was the 4-8-2s would generally provide faster results than the 2-6-6-2 Z Class Mallets in similar use.

Common with several Mountain types on a number of railroads was that the heavier-than-normal main rod was connected to the third driving axle. This design essentially limited the K-3s to a top operating speed of 35 mph. This was considered acceptable in an era when the "drag freight" mentality had not yet given way to the race for speed in freight service. This concept soon gripped American railroads as the Super Power locomotives began operating at much greater speeds.

Because of the heavy main rod's throw, these engines really pounded the track through what is termed "dynamic augment." This means that the entire driving set lifted off and was then thrown back down on the rail just a tiny bit at each power stroke of the pistons. This was enough to cause problems with track structure and increased maintenance costs. For this reason, the K-3s were usually operated at, or below, their 35 mph upper range, and were soon outmoded as "fast" freight haulers.

The K-3s had only 63-inch drivers in recognition of their slower operating speed, and need for power over speed, as opposed to the other 4-8-2s that were designed for passenger service. Logically, they were the heaviest of the N&W Mountain types at 401,900 pounds engine weight. They had 225 psi boiler pressure and exerted a rated 68,800 pounds of tractive effort.

The K-3s were good in slow speed freight work, and they could handle manifest freights of lower tonnage on the low-grade areas of the system. However, when used in manifest freight work the K-1- and K-2-Classes could out-do them handily. The K-1/2 locomotives also rode well and did not pound the track at higher speeds, as did the K-3s.

When the A-Class simple articulated 2-6-6-4 arrived starting in 1936-37, it was the logical replacement for the K-3s for fast freight. An ideal Super Power locomotive, the A-Class was better than the K-3s in speed, tonnage by orders of magnitude, and caused less damage to track structure.

However, the glut of traffic that came to N&W as the run up to World War II began, and the lack of sufficient numbers of A-Class 2-6-6-4s to take the business, the K-3s continued to work until six were sold to the RF&P in 1944, and four to the

D&RGW in 1945, to supplant those lines' heavy power during the final phases of World War II. RF&P (and D&RGW) found them equally problematic and sold them to the Wheeling and Lake Erie. When W&LE was merged into the Nickel Plate Road, they went to their third owner.

The K-1, 2, and 2a types were the primary locomotives for N&W's name trains in the mountainous territory across western Virginia and West Virginia, between Crewe and Williamson. They also ran the heavy Southern Railway trains operating over N&W between Monroe and Bristol, Virginia (which included the Blue Ridge and Alleghany grades). The Shenandoah Valley line's passenger, mixed, and even freight trains were pulled by these locomotives regularly, and the class operated the passenger trains on this line to their very end.

The classes also often handled the heaviest name trains between Norfolk and Crewe as well, and in the west their territory extended to Cincinnati and Columbus.

As J-Class 4-8-4s became the mainline power of choice, the 4-8-2s continued their work on the Shenandoah Valley trains, and on the Portsmouth-Columbus-Cincinnati trains, both the passenger and freight. They also handled secondary trains east of Crewe, Virginia.

Interestingly, the K-2 and K-2a-Classes were both given the same streamlining as the J-Class, and if one looks quickly at a photo of one of these locomotives in this streamlined dress, it is very easy to say that one is looking at a "J" until the number of drivers are counted. It was a remarkable makeover for these World War I-era engines. They entered the streamlined era *en masse* and without missing a beat, and worked to the end.

The N&W was successful in using the 4-8-2 type, not only during the 1920-1930s era after introduction, but even to the end of the line as they worked beside Js and As. They do not, however receive the same coverage in this book as the A-, J-, and Y-Classes, since their overall contribution to the traffic flow of the era was decidedly smaller than the three big classes noted. They are best remembered today as streamlined "little sisters" to the Js.

### Specifications - K-2 & K-2a (As of June 3, 1938)

**Weights:**

| | |
|---|---|
| Lead Truck: | 51,500 lbs. |
| Drivers: | 243,000 lbs. |
| Trailer: | 57,500 lbs |
| Total Engine | 352,000 lbs. |
| Tender: | 22-ton/16,000 gallons or 26-ton/18,000 gal. |

**Wheels:**

| | |
|---|---|
| Leading Truck: | 33 inches |
| Drivers: | 69 inches |
| Trailer: | 43 inches |
| Cylinders: | 25x30 inches |
| Boiler Pressure: | 220 pounds per square inch |

**Heating Surface:**

| | |
|---|---|
| Flues: | 4,118 sq. ft. |
| Firebox: | 335 sq. ft. |
| Arch Tubes: | 34 sq. ft. |
| Superheater: | 1,085 sq. ft. |
| Total | 5,572 sq. ft. |
| Grate Area: | 73 sq. ft. |
| Firebox Inside: | 92-¼ in. x 114-5/8 in. |
| Tractive Effort: | 58,000 lbs. |

*K-1 No. 107 rides the Shaffer's Crossing turntable in this nice N&W official photo. Shining black and ready for its portrait, this is a handsome locomotive by any measure. An interesting feature of this photo is that it shows the tender of No. 107 fitted with a fuel oil tank for use during the extended coal strikes of 1949 The strike resulted in temporary elimination of many trains throughout the country due to severe coal shortages. (N&W Ry. Photo, TLC Collection)*

K-1 No. 107 has charge of the three-car Lynchburg-Durham local, stopped for business at the modernized Lynchburg Union Station in July 1954. (H. Reid Photo)

K-1 No. 112 rounds a curve on the Blue Ridge grade with a westbound local freight in December 1957. Built at Roanoke in 1917, it first handled the best of the name trains over the mountain territory. By the time of this photo, the engine was downgraded to local freight work. It was retired in October 1957, just 10 months after this shot was taken. (William E. Warden Photo, TLC Collection)

Another K-1, this time No. 113, is pulling another of the Lynchburg-Durham trains in August 1947. On that date, there were two sets of trains daily between the two cities. (H. Reid Photo)

No. 115, the last built of the K-1-Class, is heading a Roanoke-bound train at Winston-Salem, North Carolina, at that city's Union Station at 1:50 p.m., October 10, 1954. (TLC Collection)

K-2 No. 118 is at Hagerstown, Maryland, working passenger or fast freight on the Shenandoah line in May 1935, before its 1946 streamlining. After the streamlining, the two air pumps were taken from the side and hidden behind the cowl, up front behind the ladders. (Bruce Fales photo, Joe Schmitz Collection)

No. 119, a K-2-Class, is seen here on March 6, 1950, at Cincinnati Union Station, ready to take The Cavalier eastbound. The K-2- and K-2a-Classes got their streamlined dress in 1945-46 to match the Js, giving almost all N&W's passenger fleet the modern look. (Joe Schmitz Photo, TLC Collection)

98

*Streamlined K-2 No. 120 has a short local train in tow at Bedford, Virginia, in 1954. (John Krause photo, TLC Collection)*

*Below: This portrait of K-2 No. 121 shows the locomotive just as it arrived from the builder, but following some additional work. It was probably taken after refurbishing at Roanoke shops. Many roads used the white paint on the drivers, but it was soon obscured by road grime. (TLC Collection)*

*Bottom: Roanoke shops took this fine builder's photo of K-2 No. 125 just after the streamlining was added in 1946. One has to be careful not to confuse this photo with one of a J-Class 4-8-4! (N&W Ry. Photo, TLC Collection)*

No. 123, one of Alco's products of 1919, is handling a local train at Elliston, Virginia, in the snow in the 1930s. (N&W Ry. Photo, TLC Collection)

No. 123 is seen again, this time in its streamlined dress, on the point double-heading with a J-Class 4-8-4 on the eastbound Cavalier at Kenova, West Virginia, in February 1956. One would hardly believe it was the same locomotive. What a difference clothes make. ( H. H. Harwood photo).

*K-2a No 130 is on the ready track at Shenandoah, Virginia, on Sept. 5, 1954, probably next out on a local freight. (TLC Collection)*

*K-2a No. 131 pauses at night on the "New York Train" at Waynesboro, Virginia, in 1958, at the very end of steam on this train. It had sleepers that connected with the PRR to New York at Hagerstown, thus the name. (William Gordon photo)*

No. 133 is rounding a very sharp curve at Portsmouth, Ohio, with a long passenger train (see the rear cars to the left) in 1954. The streamlined K-2s and K-2a's often had duty on trains originating and terminating between Columbus and Portsmouth, and Cincinnati and Portsmouth. (TLC Collection)

This is a good right side view of No. 136 as it pauses between assignments at the Portsmouth, Ohio, yard about 1950. (TLC Collection)

Freight hauler 4-8-2 K-3 No. 201 is shown in this left side profile. Note the 1930s treatment: graphited smoke box, small cab lettering, etc. A really powerful looking machine. The photo shows clearly the connection of the main rod to the third axle, characteristic of these engines. (TLC Collection)

This builder's portrait shows the right side of a K-3, this time No. 205. By any measure a compact and powerful design. (TLC Collection)

At the Shaffer's Crossing engine terminal, No. 207 is ready for some freight work at the very opening of our time period, September 1, 1930. The engine is only seven years old at this time. (TLC Collection)

This is former N&W K-3 No. 205, but here is numbered RF&P No. 520 at Richmond's Acca yard in 1946 in freight work on the RF&P. (TLC Collection)

# 10: S Class – 0-8-0s

The N&W started its locomotive roster by acquiring 0-6-0 engines designated for switching service, and eventually acquired some 0-8-0s. However, during most of the period under consideration in this book (after scrapping earlier switchers), it used downgraded road engines of the 2-8-0, 4-8-0, and 2-6-6-2 types for regular shifter and switching duties, as well as the giant Y-classes, when needed.

It was not until 1950 that the railroad opted for the purpose-built 0-8-0 switcher, when N&W acquired a fleet of 30 secondhand 0-8-0s from neighboring C&O. N&W liked them so well that it then built an additional 45 duplicates at Roanoke Shops through 1953. In fact, the class was the last steam built at Roanoke, and the last steam locomotive-type built for any Class I railroad in the United States.

Back in 1885, Roanoke Machine Works built three 0-6-0 switchers for N&W and added six more in 1893. These were gone by World War I, except for a few that became tank engines for shop work (lasting to 1926). N&W subsequently bought 13 more 0-6-0s, but by the early 1900s, these were not powerful enough for the work of shifting long cuts of coal cars, when coal became the predominate commodity for N&W. That is when N&W began converting some 2-8-0s to 0-8-0s, and also started using unconverted engines for yard work. Later, as Y-Classes and others displaced many 4-8-0s from road work, some were downgraded to switcher duties. About the only modification made was the addition of larger footboards on the pilots.

Eventually, N&W had a fleet of W-6 0-8-0 tank-style engines that had been converted from W-1 and W-2 2-8-0 classes. These served as shop switchers in Roanoke, Williamson, Bluefield, and possibly some other locales. Many were not retired

and scrapped until the 1950s, with the last in 1958.

However, the real story of the switching-type locomotive on N&W was played out during the last 10 years of steam. As it happened, neighbor C&O purchased a large order of new steam locomotives that was delivered in 1948. At that time C&O, like N&W, was completely wedded to steam motive power. Among the locomotives in that large order from various builders was a group of 30 Class C-16 0-8-0 switchers.

C&O had helped pioneer the 0-8-0 as a switcher-type in the early days of the 20th century for heavy coal switching work at Clifton Forge, Virginia, and bought many over the following years. The engines in the C&O C-16-Class delivered in 1948 were virtual duplicates of those in a fleet that C&O already operated. Then suddenly, C&O gave up its pro-steam stance and in 1949, installed a large number of diesel switchers, at first claiming that it was replacing steam only in yard service. Of course, this quickly led to complete dieselization of the road by 1956. The 0-8-0s were the first replaced, starting in 1949. Thus, by 1950, C&O owned a large number of new 0-8-0s, for which it had no use. The solution was to sell them at bargain prices to nearby N&W and Virginian, which were still steam-oriented, in 1950.

N&W bought the 30 ex-C&O 0-8-0s for the bargain price of $45,000 each and classed them S-1. They retained the C&O road numbers of 255-284, since they didn't duplicate anything in the N&W roster. The switchers were modified by N&W with the addition of a second air pump and relocation of some details to accommodate it. The tenders were changed by adding water capacity by means of a clerestory behind the coal bunker.

During the early months of operation, N&W employees and operating personnel liked the S-1 0-8-0s so well the mechanical department put Roanoke shops to work building 45

*Not really a part of the main N&W fleet, but nonetheless a member of its roster, was tiny 0-4-0T No. 3, which was used for internal switching work at the Radford crosstie treatment plant. It was built by Vulcan in 1916 and acquired secondhand by N&W from Inland Steel. It was retired May 17, 1957. The photo was taken at the Radford plant July 29, 1949. (A. A. Thieme photo, TLC Collection)*

*No. 12 is typical of the N&W's 0-8-0 shop shifters that were mainly used at Roanoke, Williamson, and Bluefield. It is seen here at Roanoke riding the turntable in the early 1950s. Retired in April 1958, it began life as an 2-8-0 road engine, built by Baldwin in 1899. (TLC Collection)*

more. They were virtual duplicates of the ex-C&O engines. One noticeable feature of the N&W-built engines was the welded sides of the tender and a built-up coal bunker. These were given class S-1a and road numbers 200-244. The last one was rolled out in December 1953, and thus was the last product of the Roanoke Shops, closed out the long history of N&W's home-built steam locomotive fleet.

Put to work beside the S-1s, these stout switchers carried on until both classes were largely retired in 1958-59, as the steam era on N&W drew to a close. However, seven of these were renumbered (to 290-296) because of a conflict with diesel numbers, and continued actively until the final dropping of steam fires in 1960.

It can be said that N&W's greatest era of steam switching work was carried out in the last 10 years of steam. As C&O had done before them, but on a much larger scale, when N&W finally dieselized, it was left with almost new steam locomotives of several modern types, not the least of which was the S-1 and S-1a 0-8-0s.

*Builder's photo from Roanoke Shops showing the left side view of the S-1a-Class. (TLC Collection)*

In 1947 N&W experimented with what was termed an "Automatic" switcher. The boiler was constructed to accomplish re-circulation, more complete combustion of gasses, and elimination of exhaust smoke. This served to conserve fuel and comply with smoke abetment laws. New controls also supplied the boiler with water and operated the coal stoker automatically when required. This allowed the engine's boiler to function with a minimum of human intervention, and supposedly regulated it so that it reached maximum efficiency.

Two Class M-2 4-8-0s (Nos. 1100 and 1112) were rebuilt this way. They were extensively scrutinized by N&W's mechanical department until the whole idea was abandoned in 1951 and the two locomotives scrapped. Contributing to this must have been the arrival and success of the ex-C&O S-1 0-8-0s, and construction of the N&W S-1a 0-8-0s.

Unmistakable in appearance, with a large skyline casing on top of the boiler and flat front-end, they looked somewhat top-heavy and ungainly. It was another of the many ideas and experiments that were being tried in American railroading in the latter years of steam.

*This left side view of No. 1100 demonstrates its ungainly and top-heavy appearance. Roanoke, ca. 1948. (TLC Collection)*

S-1 No. 266 is seen in a broadside view at Radford, Virginia, on December 30, 1952. Evident in this view is the compact and powerful appearance these engines gave. Note that the tender has been modified from its C&O appearance to comport with those on the new S-1a-Class, still being built at Roanoke when this photo was taken. The clerestory added to the top of the tender behind the coal bunker, to increase water capacity, is clearly seen in this photo (C. W. Witbeck photo, TLC Collection)

Working at Columbus in the early 1950s, S-1a No. 231 is seen in left profile. (Don Etter photo, Jay Williams Collection)

At Suffolk, Virginia, in 1958, S-1a No. 255 has just had its coal bunker filled by a conveyor-type automatic coaler. (H. Reid photo, TLC Collection)

No. 239 gets a chance to exercise outside the Portsmouth yard about 1954 while pulling a transfer move in reverse at Coal Grove, Ohio. (Gene Huddleston photo, Ron Rosenberg Collection)

S-1a No. 242 awaits assignment at Columbus, at night, in the mid-1950s. (TLC Collection)

A rare overhead view shows the top on an S-1a tender at Portsmouth, Ohio. (Jay Williams Collection)

## 11: Steam Turbine Electric

No treatment of N&W steam motive power could be presented without briefly discussing the famous, or infamous, Steam-Turbine-Electric locomotive No. 2300, known as the "Jawn Henry." N&W built a single unit of this concept - a completely new technology - that would allow it to continue using coal as a fuel for its locomotives. It was not successful.

Progress in technology and scientific development, accelerated by World War II, encouraged railroads to consider alternatives to the reciprocating steam locomotive as a means of motive power. The direction taken by almost all railroads was to adopt wholesale the improved diesel-electric locomotive. It had been proven in the 1930s, and by the mid-1940s, was poised to replace steam in just over a decade. This was certainly the most drastic change in railroad operations in the century, and its ramifications were broad.

The diesel engine driving an electrical generator, which in turn powered traction motors slung over the axles of the locomotive, was to prove vastly more effective and efficient than reciprocating steam locomotives in all ranges and types of service. Not only were railway operations better facilitated, but railroads experienced faster turn-around and availability of locomotives, as well as extreme ease of maintenance, as compared with steam power. This would ultimately allow downsizing of shops and numbers of staff, resulting in reduced costs.

Because of the lack of dynamic augment (see page 95), the diesel was much easier on the track structure than steam, which pounded the roadbed. This abuse required constant maintenance, however with diesels, smaller maintenance-of-way forces were possible at a substantial savings. Since diesels were standardized designs with off-the-shelf availability of the unit and all its component parts, maintenance and replacement were akin to the automotive concept.

Even with all these advantages, certain railroads and industries were still heavily invested in coal as a primary fuel. These roads, of course, were resistant to diesels, which eliminated any such close connection. The three "Pocahontas Roads," N&W, C&O, and Virginian, were the primary carriers of coal in the eastern U. S. B&O and PRR were also heavily involved in coal transport. Of these, the three Pocahontas lines resisted dieselization most strongly.

In an effort to develop a type of motive power that still used coal, but had all the advantages of the diesel, C&O developed a steam-turbine-electric locomotive in conjunction with Baldwin Locomotive Works and General Electric Corporation. Its infamous M-1 class of three gargantuan locomotives was delivered December 1947-January 1948, to be showcased on a new, ultra-luxury Washington-Cincinnati passenger train. The train was cancelled because of economic issues and declining passenger traffic. The new steam turbine-electrics were put in regular passenger operation in 1948-49. They proved an abject failure for numerous reasons: as a new technology they didn't have the

This is a mechanical diagram of the N&W No. 2300. Note the coal bunker in the nose, controls in the center in front of the water-tube boiler, followed toward the rear by the turbine and electric generator. Water was in the tender that trailed the main unit. (TLC Collection)

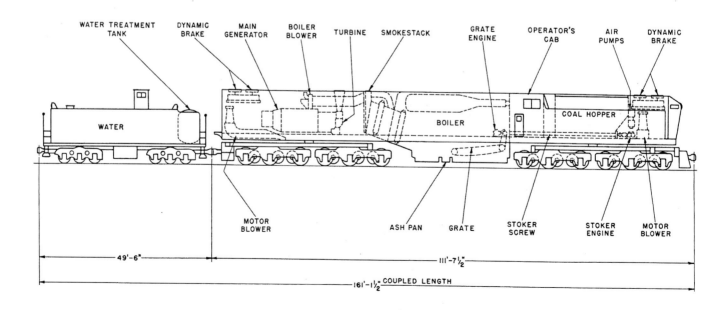

appropriate testing, and were thrown into a railway system that was solely geared to reciprocating steam in its maintenance, shops, skills, training, thinking, etc. After a year they were quietly scrapped. Shortly, the diesels began to arrive, ending steam on C&O in late 1956.

Across the mountains at Roanoke, the N&W was very mindful of this experience and was, in fact, concurrently developed a very similar locomotive with Baldwin-Lima-Hamilton (the successor to Baldwin and Lima), Westinghouse Electric, and Babcock & Wilcox, the boiler designers. Although this concept work began about 1947 - the same time that the C&O locomotives were being built - it did not produce a single locomotive until May 1954, when Baldwin's old works in Philadelphia completed N&W No. 2300. It, too, was fired by coal, which generated steam to turn a turbine, powering a generator to send electricity to traction motors. Like the C&O engine, it was a steam-turbine-electric. Unlike C&O, it had a water-tube boiler (whereas C&O's had been fire-tube). The layout of the locomotive was similar, with a coal bunker in the nose, cab next, and then the boiler, followed by the turbine and generator. A water tender trailed the main engine. At 161 feet in total length (including water tender), it was a bit longer than the 154 feet of the C&O's locomotive.

Rather than throwing it into a high profile service, N&W undertook extensive and methodical testing with its dynamometer car and used the locomotive in a variety of freight service. It was found that in certain service, it could do as well, or better, than the famous Y-6 2-8-8-2s that were the backbone of N&W coal traffic, and. . . could generally do the same work with less coal consumption.

During this period of testing, a great deal was printed about the locomotive, both in the railroad trade press and public media. The informal name of "Jawn Henry" was given to the new engine in memory of the great "Paul Bunyan of the Rails." Ironically, his legend was born on the C&O, not the N&W. Nonetheless, it was a great name and a great way to attract public attention.

There were problems, and after the testing period, the Jawn Henry was retired and scrapped. It simply could not compete with the many advantages of the diesel. Work continued on the idea of a gas-turbine-electric locomotive by N&W, C&O, B&O, PRR and other railroads and industries for some time in a consortium called the Bituminous Coal Research Institute. Ultimately nothing came of it. The best design that reached operational capability was on the Union Pacific, whose huge turbine-electrics used a low grade of oil as fuel. They achieved a modicum of success, but could not overcome the benefits of diesel-electric.

The two years or so of the turbine on the N&W were exciting and dramatic, but they came to naught. Had C&O's and N&W's concept been tried 20 years earlier, before the diesel-electric had been perfected to such a high degree, there could very possibly have been a period when the steam-turbine-electric type would have achieved success--but it was not to be.

This official N&W photo shows the gleaming black Jawn Henry soon after its delivery in May 1954. (N&W Ry. Photo, TLC Collection)

In actual service during its period of testing, the 2300 has a built-up bunker at the top of its coal space in which mechanical department workers rode to monitor testing. Photos of the locomotive usually show the N&W dynamometer car behind it, but in this case it is absent. However, there is a second water tender. These approaching and going away photos at Elliston, Virginia, in 1954 give a good impression of how the giant looked to bystanders. (Jay Williams Collection)

*This photo, taken in August 1954, shows Jawn Henry tackling the Christiansburg grade up Alleghany Mountain, with the usual set of mechanical department personnel in the space above the coal bunker to monitor performance. (E. P. Street photo, H. H. Harwood Collection)*

*Jawn Henry is powering manifest freight No. 85 at Shawsville, Virginia, in August 1954. It was believed that this locomotive would prove ideal for fast freight service, but it did not meet expectations. (E. P. Street photo, H. H. Harwood Collection)*

*Engineer and fireman are shown at the controls of the 2300, which were in a word: simple, especially compared with a standard reciprocating steam engine. (N&W photos TLC Collection)*

*Three mechanical department personnel are on the roof as the Jawn Henry powers an empty coal train, with the dynamometer car in tow, at Elliston, Virginia. (H. Reid photo, TLC Collection)*

*J-Class No. 603 passes Jawn Henry as the latter pauses on the main line at Elliston, Virginia. The 2300 has two water tenders and the dynamometer car ahead of its train. (G. C. Corey Photo, Ron Rosenberg Collection)*

*After testing and a brief stint as a pusher, No. 2300 sits forlorn and decrepit-looking in the scrap line at Roanoke on January 22, 1959 as it awaits its end. (TLC Collection)*